TOWARD FAMILY MEALS

2

In the second six months of her life, you can introduce an ever-wider range of foods, tastes and textures to your baby so that by her first birthday much of what she eats is family food. As the amount of nutrients and calories your baby gets from solids increases, milk becomes a less important source of nourishment. At a year old, your baby may be eating three solid meals a day accompanied by drinks of water, diluted fruit juice, or milk. She will be taking an active role in feeding herself, too, learning the vital coordination skills necessary to pick up finger foods and use a spoon.

SIX MONTHS TO A YEAR

Your baby develops rapidly between the age of six months and a year, and this has an inevitable impact on feeding patterns. At six months most babies need support to sit and have to be held while feeding. From around eight months, they develop the strength and balance needed to sit alone and can start using a high chair. At six months, your baby has mastered the art of reaching and grabbing for a spoon, although her coordination may leave a lot to be desired, so be prepared for mess. By seven or eight months, a baby's grasp and aim are both greatly improved. Around this time, babies start to use the thumb in opposition to their fingers, enabling them to cope with finger foods and with holding a spoon and using it with slightly more precision. By the age of a year, most babies have good enough hand-eye coordination to be able to pick up a pea or raisin with precision. As coordination improves further, your baby may be able to manage drinking from a mug or cup. You can encourage your baby to develop these skills by providing plenty of practice in self-feeding.

IRON

Iron is especially important for your baby's mental and physical development. It is needed for the manufacture by the body of hemoglobin, the red pigment that transports oxygen to every cell and tissue (including the brain) and for producing the white blood cells which are vital to your baby's immune system. A shortage of iron can cause tiredness, lack of energy, lowered resistance to minor infections, and poor physical coordination. It can be difficult to meet your baby's need for iron during the early part of weaning; if you are worried that this may be a problem, talk to your pediatrician. Foods rich in iron include lean meat and whole-wheat bread and cereals; other good sources are leafy green vegetables and dried fruits.

■ Give your baby a drink of orange juice or orange or tangerine segments with meals. Vitamin C boosts iron absorption.

■ Continue giving breast or formula milk until your baby is a year old. Cow's milk is not a good source of iron.

■ Use iron-fortified breakfast cereals (check the label).

Healthy Food For Babies and Toddlers

Patsy Westcott

Consultant Margaret Lawson, Ph.D.

Alexandria, Virginia

TIME®
LIFE
BOOKS

Time-Life Books is a division of Time Life Inc.

TIME LIFE INC.

PRESIDENT AND CEO: George Artandi

TIME-LIFE CUSTOM PUBLISHING

Vice President and Publisher	Terry Newell
Vice President of Sales and Marketing	Neil Levin
Director of Acquisitions and Editorial Resources	Jennifer Pearce
Director of Creative Services	Laura McNeill
Director of Special Markets	Liz Ziehl
Project Manager	Jennie Halfant

First printing. Printed in China

TIME-LIFE is a trademark of Time Warner Inc. U.S.A.

Library of Congress Cataloging-in-Publication Data

Westcott, Patsy.
    Healthy food for babies and toddlers / Patsy Westcott.
       p. cm. -- (Time-Life health factfiles)
    Includes index.
    ISBN 0-7370-1604-3 (pbk. : alk. paper)
    1. Infants--Nutrition. 2. Toddlers--Nutrition. I. Title.
  II. Series.
  RJ216.W486   1999
  613.2'083--dc21   99-26907
                                   CIP

Books produced by Time-Life Custom Publishing are available at a special bulk discount for promotional and premium use. Custom adaptations can also be created to meet your specific marketing goals. Call 1-800-323-5255.

A Marshall Edition
Conceived, edited and designed by
Marshall Editions Ltd
161 New Bond Street
London W1Y 9PA

Dr. Margaret Lawson
Margaret Lawson, Ph.D, SRD, FRSH, is a Senior Lecturer in Pediatric Nutrition at the Institute of Child Health, London, and Head of Dietetic Services at Great Ormond Street Hospital for Children. Her research interests include the nutritional needs of sick and healthy babies and children, growth in sick babies, dietary intake and tooth decay, and the iron status of preschool children.

Note

CONTENTS

Feeding a Toddler

Food Behavior

Eating Away from Home

When Food Is a Problem

INTRODUCTION

What your child eats during the early months and years of his life lays down the foundations for his future health and wellbeing. If you can establish healthy eating habits now, you will stand your baby in good stead for the rest of his life. Your aim is to introduce solids into your baby's diet and gradually shift the balance between milk and solids until your baby is eating the same foods as the rest of the family. So, if you have not done so before, this is also the time to look at what and how you eat, too. Your baby will pick up your food habits, good and bad. If the rest of the family is eating healthy foods, your baby will enjoy them, too. If you and older brothers or sisters are constantly snacking on junk foods in between TV dinners and meals on the run, the loving preparation of a healthy meal for the baby is probably going to be wasted. Having a baby and toddler to feed is the ideal opportunity to make the whole family eat better.

COMMON QUESTIONS

Feeding a baby in the early months is relatively straightforward once you have decided whether to breast- or bottle-feed and overcome any early difficulties. But once your baby starts having solids, confusion may set in. What foods should my baby have? How do I encourage him to develop a taste for healthy, nutritious foods? How do I deal with a child who won't eat anything, or one who eats too much? Do I have to spend hours in the kitchen preparing my child's meals or can I use convenience foods? How can I prevent my child from eating too many sweet things? This book will provide the answers to all those questions, and more.

BASIC GUIDELINES

The good news is that there is nothing difficult or complicated about feeding a baby or toddler and few, if any, hard and fast rules. Most experts are now in agreement as to what constitutes a healthy diet for babies and small children (which is not the same as a healthy adult diet, see p. 107). The most important guideline is to make sure that your child's diet is varied enough to provide him with a balance of all the different nutrients he needs. The best ways to achieve this are to make sure he eats as much fresh food as possible and to keep animal fats and empty calories such as those found in candy and sugary and salty snacks to a minimum.

There is also now broad agreement over timing the introduction of solids. In the past, many babies were given solid food in the first three months of life, either because their parents saw this as a sort of "marker" that their baby was developing faster than others, or for convenience, or in the belief that solids would help a wakeful baby to sleep better. It is now clear, however, that introducing solids too early can lead to problems later, and experts agree that in most circumstances it is wise to leave solids until your baby is at least four months old, and in some families, to wait until the baby is six months.

IN THE BEGINNING

The first three chapters of this book are concerned with how, what, why, and when to feed your baby or toddler. Chapter One takes you through the early days of solid foods, offering advice on how to introduce a breast- or bottle-fed baby to solids, the equipment you may find makes life easier when you are preparing your baby's food, what kinds of foods to offer, and how to proceed as your baby begins to get increasing amounts of nourishment from solids. Menu plans are suggested, not for you to follow slavishly, although you could if you prefer to, but to give you an idea of the variety of foods – and how much food – your baby will take in the early days. Finally, the most common problems encountered by parents in these early days are addressed, and solutions offered.

AS YOUR BABY GROWS

Chapters Two and Three cover the period between about six months, by which time your baby will be accustomed to solids, and three years, when he should be eating family food at the table with the rest of the family. During this time the range of foods your child eats will expand enormously, and the tastes and textures he can cope with will increase. Here, too, sample menu plans mean you can see at-a-glance what your baby or child might like, and how much he may eat in a day.

But these are also the years when doting grandparents and older brothers and sisters may try to shower your child with candy, carbonated sugary drinks, and other so-called treats. It is virtually impossible to prevent a child from having sweet things, but you can monitor his intake. You can also make sure as many as possible of the treats he does have are healthy, and feel confident that for a child on a well-balanced diet, the odd piece of candy is not going to cause problems.

Even with the household gadgets that many of us take for granted, most parents today simply do not have the time to cook family meals from basic ingredients every day. Instead, they rely to a greater or lesser extent on some convenience foods. Again, the emphasis here is on picking the healthier options, and leaving fat- and sugar-laden ones on the supermarket shelves.

FOOD AND SOCIAL SITUATIONS

There is, of course, much more to food than simply making sure your child has his daily quota of vitamins, minerals, proteins, fat, and starches. What you eat, where and how, and your attitudes to food are as important as its nutritional value. Your baby learns about the social aspects of food from the experiences you provide, both at home and when you are out and about.

Chapter Four focuses on your child's food behavior – how to encourage acceptable table manners, how to make him one of the family at mealtimes, and how to cope with such issues as faddiness, overeating, and reluctance to give up the breast or bottle.

In some cultures children have always been welcomed in restaurants and hotels to dine with their parents and the rest of the family, and increasingly this is becoming more and more common. Today, children who have never eaten in a restaurant are the exception rather than the rule. Similarly when they are dining with friends, many parents no longer get a babysitter, but take their child along, too. And as increasing numbers of families choose to take vacations abroad, children today have the opportunity to experience an ever greater variety of national cuisines.

Chapter Five is full of practical ideas for making eating away from home relaxing and enjoyable for everyone. There is advice on choosing your venue, what to take with you when you travel, and how to make sure friends and relatives do not thwart your attempts to give your child healthy foods.

PROBLEM SOLVING

Many of the most common problems relating to food are discussed throughout the book. There are, however, many families in which one or more children has a specific food problem, such as diabetes, allergy, or intolerance. Coping in such situations can be tricky. On one hand you want your child to be as "normal" as possible; on the other he has to be aware that there are times when he can't eat what his friends are having.

Chapter Six deals with particular food problems and gives plenty of advice on how to cope.

YOU KNOW BEST

As more and more books are written about children, and more magazine articles devoted to their upbringing, there has been a tendency for parents to lose confidence in their parenting skills. This is nowhere more apparent than in relation to food, where we can feel that a prepared dish or TV dinner must somehow be "better" for our child than anything we cook. But feeding babies and small children is one area where you cannot go far wrong by sticking to the basics. A child brought up to enjoy plenty of fresh fruit and vegetables, lean meat, fish, dairy products, and whole-wheat bread and cereal products is a healthy child who will take healthy ideas about food and diet into his teen and adult life. This book will show that there is no particular mysique to feeding small children and give you the confidence that you do, indeed, know what is best for your child.

From Milk to First Solids

FROM MILK TO FIRST SOLIDS

For the first few months of life, a baby's need for nourishment is met entirely by milk, whether from the breast or from infant formula given in a bottle. However, by the time he is four to six months of age, milk alone is not enough to satisfy a baby's nutritional needs; this is the time to introduce solid foods. The process of teaching your baby to take foods and drinks from a spoon or cup rather than by sucking at the breast or a nipple is known as weaning. In addition to meeting his greater need for nutrients, introducing your baby to solids helps in the development and practice of a range of eating skills, such as biting and chewing. Last, but not least, your baby starts to acquire

THE BREAST-FED BABY

Breast milk is the perfect food and drink for your baby in the first few months of life. From birth onward the composition of breast milk continually changes to suit the needs of your growing baby. By four months, although the amount of breast milk your baby is taking may not have altered significantly, its ingredients will be perfectly balanced to meet his nutritional needs. Breast-fed babies often take to solids more readily than bottle-fed babies, perhaps because they are already used to a range of different food flavors and smells from their mother's milk.

THE BENEFITS OF BREAST-FEEDING

Nutritionally, breast milk is the most complete food your baby can have during the first few months of life. If you have managed to breast-feed your baby for all or part of this time, the health benefits will last a lifetime.

■ The nutrients in breast milk are especially easy to absorb, so breast-fed babies tend to have fewer upset stomachs.

■ Breast-feeding confers immunity to childhood infections for the first few months of life.

■ Breast-fed babies have fewer allergies than bottle-fed babies.

■ The incidence of SIDS is lower among breast-fed babies.

■ It is difficult to overfeed a breast-fed baby.

FEEDING PATTERNS

Breast-fed babies who are fed on demand feed more often and less regularly than bottle-fed babies. However, by the age of four months, most have established a fairly predictable feeding pattern. Typically, this may involve around five feeds at approximately four hourly intervals each day. However, it is not unusual for a breast-fed baby to have more frequent feeds. Many breast-fed babies start to sleep through the night from around the age of three months, though a substantial number still wake for a feed during the night.

WEIGHT GAIN IN BREAST-FED BABIES

Breast-fed babies naturally tend to gain weight in a less predictable fashion than bottle-fed babies. And, since you cannot see how much milk your baby is taking at any one feed – as you can if he is taking milk from a bottle – some breast-feeding mothers worry that their babies may not be getting enough nourishment. Your baby is likely to be taking enough milk if he:

- is fed on demand and unrestrictedly; he will come off the breast when he has had enough, whether that is after five minutes or half an hour

- has six really wet diapers in 24 hours

- seems alert and happy

- seems settled; he may not be sleeping through the night yet, but neither is he crying for no apparent reason

- is gaining weight in general, even though the amount varies from week to week and there are some weeks when he gains little or nothing.

THE NEED FOR SOLIDS

For the first four to six months of life, breast milk or infant formula provides all the nutrients your baby needs. By six months, however, solids are needed to provide your baby with energy, protein, and vitamins A and D. Although the iron in breast milk is more easily absorbed than that found in cow's milk or formula, after the age of six months the amount obtained from breast milk alone is not enough to meet your baby's needs. Extra zinc and copper are needed, too.

TIMING THE INTRODUCTION OF SOLIDS

Your breast-fed baby's need for different sources of nutrients coincides with a growing interest in the outside world. Your baby may seem less interested in feeding from the breast, stopping sucking after a few minutes' feeding or trying to sit up and have a look around after the first few sucks. If you breast-feed at the table, your baby may show an interest in what you are eating, he may watch intently as you lift a forkful of food to your mouth or even try to take some food from your plate.

All babies have growth spurts – periods when they need extra nutrients to fuel growth and development. Breast-feeding works by a system of supply and demand so, when a breast-fed baby is going through a growth spurt, he will demand feeds more frequently for a day or so.

A convenient time to think about starting to introduce solids is any time after the age of four months when your baby has a growth spurt and starts to demand more frequent breast-feeds, indicating an increase in appetite.

THE BOTTLE-FED BABY

The majority of infant formulas are based on cow's milk and designed to be as close as possible to breast milk. If you are unable to breast-feed your baby, or do not want to do so exclusively for the first few months, you can be sure your baby is getting all he needs nutritionally from a formula. Although your baby may seem hungry or to be growing especially fast, it is wise to delay introducing solids before the age of four to six months as a baby's digestive system is not mature enough to cope with them until then.

If your baby does seem particularly hungry before this age, there are formulas designed to resemble breast milk but containing more protein than first feeds. One of these may satisfy your baby's hunger. You should never make a bottle with a higher concentration of formula than recommended, nor add crumbled zwieback or baby rice to bottle feeds.

FEEDING PATTERNS

Right from the start, bottle-fed babies tend to adopt a more regular feeding pattern than breast-fed babies. Formula milk contains more protein than breast milk, so babies tend to be satisfied longer between feeds. At the same time, the type of protein found in formula milks tends to take longer to pass through the baby's digestive system. This again makes for a longer interval between feed times.

GIVING SOLIDS EARLY

Doctors or health visitors do not recommend solids before four months. However, there are two circumstances in which they may agree to you giving them early:

■ if your baby is very big and hungry, and still demanding food every two hours at three months

■ if your baby was premature, solids should not normally be given until 16 weeks after his due date. However these babies are often hungry, and early solids may be suggested.

Just like anyone else's, your baby's appetite will fluctuate to a certain extent from one day to another and from one feed to the next. However, by around four months most bottle-fed babies are having approximately five 7 ounce (200 ml) feeds a day. These are usually spaced at around four hourly intervals. A bottle-fed baby will probably be sleeping through the night.

THE NEED FOR SOLIDS

By the age of four to six months, the iron stores with which a baby is born begin to dwindle. Cow's milk is a poor source of iron, and the type of iron contained in baby formulas tends to be less well absorbed than the iron in breast milk. This is one important reason why bottle-fed babies of this age need to start being introduced to other foods.

As your baby grows, increasing amounts of milk are needed in order to supply the energy necessary for growth and development. However, a baby's stomach can only hold so much, and there will come a point when, even drinking as much as possible at each feed, there are not enough calories to supply energy for growth. This is the time for solids to be introduced.

TIMING THE INTRODUCTION OF SOLIDS

The time to start thinking about introducing solids is around four months if your baby starts to appear dissatisfied with the amount of milk he is getting from the bottle. He may stop sucking on the nipple, or start to gum it rather than drink any milk. If your baby suddenly starts wanting an extra feed having previously been perfectly happy with just five a day, still seems hungry after drinking a full bottle, or starts waking up again in the night for a feed after previously sleeping through, you will know it is time for solids.

WHEN TO WEAN

Every baby is an individual – so the time to think about starting solids is when your baby seems ready rather than according to a rigid set date. In the past, mothers were often advised to start giving their babies cereal as early as six weeks of age, and even quite recently experts used to advise mothers to give babies tastes of solid foods at three months. It is now thought that this is both unnecessary and potentially harmful.

WHEN TO START

The exact time at which a baby needs to start solids varies, but it is inadvisable to start before four months of age. By six months, your baby should be eating a mixture of different foods. Large quantities of solids are not necessary at this age since milk continues to be the main source of nourishment for the first six to nine months of life. Take your time and be guided by your baby.

READY FOR SOLIDS

Think about solids if your baby:

■ is at least four months and has doubled his birthweight

■ no longer seems satisfied by milk feeds

■ starts demanding feeds more frequently

■ starts waking at night after sleeping through

■ is taking an interest in what you are eating

■ is putting things such as a rattle in his mouth and gnawing them

■ can keep a runny puree in his mouth

WINDOW OF OPPORTUNITY

All babies have "sensitive periods" during which they are ready to learn a new activity – such as taking food from a spoon. If this opportunity is missed, the child may find it difficult to acquire the new skill later.

Several factors coincide at around four months, making it a favorable time to introduce solids. By this age a baby's birthweight has usually doubled, and the corresponding need for energy and nutrients has increased to the point that it can no longer be met by milk alone. By this age, too, the digestive tract and kidneys have matured enough to cope with foods other than milk. And some babies are sleeping through the night without waking for an extra feed.

At four months, your baby has the nerve and muscle coordination to sit supported in a chair. Also, his inbuilt reflex to push out solid food – and other objects – with his tongue (a reflex intended to prevent choking in the early months) has begun to disappear.

In addition, your baby can now hold his head up which, in turn, means that solid food can be moved from the front to the back of his mouth and swallowed.

STRIKING A BALANCE

Weaning too early or too late can result in behavioral and health problems and family stress.

Too early

■ May predispose your baby to allergies

■ May cause your baby to reject solids, paving the way for later battles over food

■ May strain the digestive system and kidneys

■ May lead to a lack of the vital nutrients in milk

Too late

■ Can make it hard for your baby to learn the skills of biting and chewing

■ May make it difficult for your baby to enjoy solids

■ Will deprive your baby of vital nutrients, especially iron.

HAZARDS OF EARLY SOLIDS

A baby's digestive system does not contain the necessary enzymes to deal with solid food. Giving a baby under four months solids may increase the risk of developing allergies such as asthma, eczema, and hayfever later. This is because the gut cannot screen out large protein molecules that can set up reactions.

■ A persistent cough is more common in babies given solids before 12 weeks.

■ Persistent diarrhea, caused by intolerance of gluten, a protein found in wheat-based foods, is also more common in babies given solids too early.

■ Giving early solids strains a baby's kidneys, increasing the risk of dehydration.

■ A baby who is fed solids too early can gain too much weight. This a health hazard. Overweight babies may grow into overweight adults with the extra risks of diabetes, heart disease, and other serious health problems.

STARTING OUT

All your baby really needs when you start giving solids is a clean, shallow, plastic spoon, an unbreakable bowl, and a bib. Later a cup with a spout for drinks is a good idea, although you can use an ordinary cup from the start. A highchair is not essential in the early stages of weaning, but having one once your baby is taking more solid food means that he can join the rest of the family at the table for meals. There are several other pieces of equipment that make life easier, many of which you may have in your kitchen already.

FEEDING EQUIPMENT

■ A small, shallow weaning spoon for first tastes.

■ A bigger teaspoon and fork, preferably plastic (this is gentle on gums).

■ An angled spoon and fork, which are easier for a baby to use.

■ A small shallow plastic bowl.

■ A bowl with a suction pad for when your baby is at the "dropping everything on the floor" stage; this also means he does not have to chase the bowl around his highchair tray.

■ A bowl with a false bottom that you can fill with warm water to keep food warm.

■ A spouted cup – the spout prevents spills if the cup tips over and is easier at first when your baby has only been used to sucking. Two handles are easier to cope with than one.

■ A cup that is weighted at the bottom, making it harder to knock over.

■ Bibs: a plastic-backed terrycloth bib for early tastes; one with sleeves for older babies helps to minimize the mess; a molded plastic bib with a trough for catching pieces of dropped food is a good idea for older babies and toddlers.

■ A plastic sheet to protect the floor: this is particularly useful if the floor is carpeted, less so if you have a wipe-clean surface.

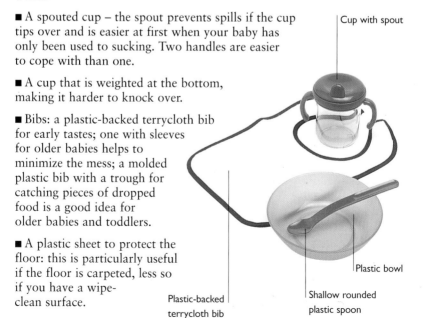

Cup with spout

Plastic bowl

Plastic-backed
terrycloth bib

Shallow rounded
plastic spoon

FOOD PREPARATION EQUIPMENT

■ A liquidizer or food processor to mash or puree food to a thin, semiliquid consistency. This is especially useful for processing bigger amounts of food to freeze in batches.

■ A small hand blender or food mill with different cutting disks for different textures for small quantities of food.

■ A strainer for pureeing smaller quantities or separating the seeds and skin from fruit and vegetables.

■ A grater.

■ A small saucepan reserved for heating portions of baby food, particularly useful for commercially prepared baby foods and for portions of food that have been frozen.

■ A small metal steaming disk to place over the top of an ordinary saucepan or a multitiered steamer so you can cook several different foods at once.

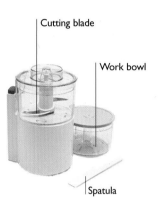

Cutting blade

Work bowl

Spatula

HIGH CHAIRS

At first you may feed your baby on your lap or as he sits in a baby chair, but from the age of about six months a highchair is useful. There are several different types. A folding chair is a good idea if space is limited, but it must be sited on a stable surface. Make sure, too, that the frame locks rigidly to prevent it from folding up while your baby is in it or trapping his fingers.

A multifunctional model that converts into a separate low chair and table may be useful for longer (but less convenient if you have a second child fairly quickly). There are also models that convert into baby-walkers or swings. Whichever type you choose, make sure there are hooks for a clip-on safety harness.

Padded backrest to support your baby's head

Wipe-clean tray with a rim to catch spills

Wipe-clean seat

Sturdy construction

Converts into a low table when the seat is removed

STERILIZATION ROUTINES

When you first start your baby on solid foods, you should sterilize the bowls, dishes, and spoons you use for feeding, using the same methods of sterilization you would use for bottles and nipples. In practice, it is impossible to sterilize every piece of equipment you use for preparing and cooking your baby's food, and in any case once your baby is crawling around and picking things up from the floor it is rather pointless to sterilize spoons, bowls, and other utensils.

SAFETY FIRST

To ensure your baby's safety, wash all the utensils and equipment you use for feeding your baby in hot, soapy water and rinse thoroughly in hot water. Before preparing your baby's food, clean all work surfaces. Wash your hands with soap before you start food preparation and before feeding your baby, as well as before and after changing his diaper.

Warning

Because warm milk is a breeding ground for bacteria, you should continue to sterilize bottles and nipples in the usual way until your baby is a year old.

Sterilizing tank

Nipple holder

Lid

Sterilizing fluid

Sterilizing tablets

Bottle cover

Nipple

Bottle

METHODS OF STERILIZATION

Type	Advantages	Method
Chemical	The cheapest option if you have to sterilize several bottles a day. Sterilized bottles are always available.	Half fill the sterilization unit or a plastic bucket with cold water, and add a sterilizing tablet or liquid. Wash the baby's spoons and bowls, and put them into the container, making sure they are completely submerged. Leave them for the specified time. Utensils can stay in the solution until it is time to feed your baby. Rinse in cooled boiled water to get rid of the taste of the chemicals.
Steaming	Fast and effective, although less useful if space is at a premium in your kitchen: even the smallest units take up space.	Steam reaches much higher temperatures than those achieved by boiling water, making this a very effective way of getting rid of bacteria. Wash everything you intend to sterilize first to remove all traces of food. You can buy steam sterilizers that take about 10 minutes.
Boiling	Requires no initial outlay and takes up no extra space.	Place all the equipment in a large saucepan, making sure it is completely submerged, cover with a lid, and boil for 25 minutes.
Microwave	Fast and effective.	You can buy microwave sterilizers for bottles that work the same way as steam sterilization except that they go inside the microwave. Check that the unit will fit inside your microwave; some sterilizers are too large for smaller models.
Dishwasher	If you have a dishwasher already, this method involves no extra outlay or any more time: you would be running the machine in any case.	The water in a dishwasher is much hotter than it would be if you washed utensils by hand, but the exact temperatures vary. Dishwashers are adequate for sterilizing if the water temperature reaches at least 180°F (82°C), so check your manufacturer's instructions. A dishwasher will also dry bottles and utensils in the drying cycle.

PREPARING FIRST FOODS

Since your baby is used to drinking fluids, he is likely to accept his first tastes of solids more readily if they are smooth and semiliquid in consistency. At first try fairly bland foods that can easily be reduced to a runny puree. Pureed vegetables or fruit and baby rice mixed with a little expressed breast milk, formula milk, or cooled boiled water all make ideal first tastes. Your baby will usually only try a teaspoon or so; at this stage he is getting used to the taste and texture of solids rather than needing them for their nutritional value.

COOKING YOUR BABY'S FOOD

As the amounts of food you give your baby are so small at first, you may find it easier and cheaper to make it yourself rather than buy it ready made. Wash all fruit and vegetables well and peel them; carefully remove any seeds, stones, or indigestible fibrous parts. Cut them into small pieces.

To make it easier for your baby to digest at this stage, fruit and vegetables – with the exception of ripe bananas – should be cooked until they are very soft and easy to puree. Suitable cooking methods include boiling, steaming, stewing, baking, or microwaving, but avoid frying and roasting, as they involve fat. You should not add sugar or salt to the water you use to cook in.

■ **Boiling:** Prepare the fruit or vegetables and put them in a small saucepan with enough boiling water to barely cover them. Simmer until tender. Drain the vegetables, keeping the cooking water to use for moistening the food.

■ **Steaming:** Prepare the fruit or vegetables and add them to the steamer. Steam until soft (usually around 10 minutes). Remove from the steamer, keeping the liquid.

■ **Microwaving:** Prepare fruit or vegetables as above and put in a microwave dish with just enough water to cover. Cover the dish and microwave on high for three minutes. Uncover, stir, re-cover, and cook for another two minutes or until tender. Cooking times may vary depending on the make of your microwave and the type of fruit or vegetables.

CHOOSING FIRST FOODS

Foods to try

- Baby rice or gluten-free cereal

- Pureed carrot, potato, sweet potato, or cauliflower

- Pureed avocado

- Pureed banana, stewed apple, soft ripe pear, or papaya

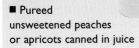

- Pureed unsweetened peaches or apricots canned in juice

Foods to avoid

- Foods with added salt or sugar including smoked or salted food such as bacon, salami, or yeast extract

- Coffee, tea, chocolate, or alcohol

- Shellfish and whole nuts

- Eggs and nut products before the age of six months

- Anything containing wheat, barley, rye, or oats before the age of six months

- Dairy products and meat, although these can be introduced when your baby is more used to solids (see pages 28-29)

2 Once the food is cooked, puree it using an electric or hand blender or by straining it. Add some expressed breast milk, formula, unsweetened fruit juice or, for vegetables, some of the cooking liquid to thin the puree.

3 Taste the food: first tastes should be smooth and very sloppy like thick cream. Make sure there are no lumps that could make your baby gag. As your baby gets used to solid foods, you can gradually increase the variety of textures and tastes.

SERVING AND STORING FOOD

Serve the food at room temperature, very slightly warmed or cold. You can safely keep pureed fruit and vegetables covered in a clean dish in the refrigerator for up to 24 hours. Alternatively, freeze any leftover puree in individual portions in an ice-cube tray. Always throw away any unfinished food that could be contaminated with saliva. To prevent contamination of the food with your saliva, do not use the same spoon for tasting the food and feeding your baby.

FIRST TASTES

Some babies take to solids enthusiastically right from the start, but most need plenty of time and lots of encouragement to learn to enjoy them. After all, solid foods smell, taste, and feel different from milk from the breast or bottle – which is all your baby has known so far. It may take your baby some time to get used to a completely different feeding technique. If you are patient and relaxed and give your baby time to get used to this strange new experience, things are likely to go smoothly.

TIMING FIRST SOLIDS

For your baby's first taste of solids, choose a quiet time of day when you are both relaxed and happy and when you are not in a rush to do other things. The noontime feed is often a good one since mornings can be busy and fraught, while by the evening your baby may be tired and less likely to welcome new experiences. If your baby is unsettled or ill, delay introducing solids until everything is back to normal.

FEEDING DO'S AND DON'TS

Do:

■ Choose a quiet, relaxed time so you can give your baby your full attention.

■ Check that the food is not too hot. This is especially important if you heat food in a microwave, since the heat-through is uneven and hot spots can develop. Follow the manufacturer's instructions, and stir and cool food before giving it to your baby.

■ Let your baby set the pace. Some babies with a large appetite may progress very quickly with solids, while others take longer.

■ Be relaxed and prepared to wait a while if your baby shows no interest: try again in a week or so.

■ Be prepared for mess. Use a bib to protect your baby's clothing – and have a cloth or roll of paper towels handy to mop up spills.

Don't:

■ Be discouraged if your baby doesn't take to solids immediately. Taking food from a spoon is a big change, so give it time.

■ Push the spoon too far into your baby's mouth.

■ Insist. If your baby cries or turns away, it's a clear sign of lack of interest – for the moment.

■ Expect your baby to eat the same amount at every feed. He may finish his bowl one day and only take a teaspoon the next.

■ Leave your baby alone while feeding – choking is a real danger.

HOW TO FEED

1 Prepare a small amount of food as described on pages 20–21. Give some breast milk or formula, then sit your baby upright on your lap, using the crook of your arm as a support. Your baby's head should be upright to make it easier for him to swallow.

2 Using a small plastic weaning spoon, scoop up a little puree and bring it gently toward your baby's lips. Some babies automatically open their mouths when you bring the spoon toward them, but if this doesn't happen, open your own mouth – your baby will usually copy you.

3 With the tip of the spoon in your baby's mouth, gently angle the spoon upward so the puree slips off. Be careful not to push it in too far or your baby may gag and become discouraged. Most babies are puzzled at first about what to do with the food, so be patient. The first reaction is often to push the food out – but just gently scrape it up and try again.

4 If the first spoonful seems to have gone down well, offer another before giving the rest of your usual breast or bottle feed. If your baby cries or seems reluctant, however, don't force the issue. Simply continue with the rest of the breast or bottle feed and try again another day. There is no hurry: these early tastes are intended to be just that; your baby's main nourishment still comes from milk.

MAKE IT EASY ON YOURSELF

If your baby is very hungry, it is a good idea to offer a small amount of breast milk or formula before you try solids. A hungry baby is less likely to cooperate with this strange new way of taking food and may become frustrated, which could turn you both against the whole experience.

HOW MANY MEALS A DAY?

At first give your baby solids only once a day, perhaps at lunchtime. Once your baby has got used to this and appears to be enjoying solid food, you can try offering it at a second feed, perhaps at suppertime or breakfast time, following the same procedure as for the first meal. After another week or so, try offering solids at a third meal. This will get your baby into the habit of eating solid food three times a day and beginning to fit in with family meal times.

ALL ABOUT DRINKS

During the first four of five months of life while feeding from the breast or bottle, your baby's food and drink are one and the same. When you first begin weaning, breast milk or formula remains your baby's main source of calories and nutrients – and between four and six months your baby needs at least a pint (500 ml) of milk each day. However, as the amount of solid food increases, the amount of milk decreases proportionately, and you will gradually be able to reduce the number of breast or formula feeds. As your baby gets older and takes more solid food, you should offer small amounts of other fluids – this is particularly important in hot weather.

WATER IS BEST

The best drink to give – and the only drink apart from breast milk or formula your baby should have until the age of six months – is plain (tap) water. All water used to make up formula feeds or given as a drink should be boiled and cooled until then, including bottled water.

BABY DRINKS

Baby drinks are presented as an alternative to water, to broaden your baby's tastes. However, baby "herbal" and "fruit" drinks often contain undesirable amounts of sugar – a major cause of tooth decay. Labels which state "no added sugar" do not mean that a drink is sugar-free; it may naturally contain different types of sugar such as fructose (fruit sugar), glucose, dextrose, and maltose. Always read the label.

Artificial sweeteners such as saccharin and aspartame are not allowed by law in foods and drinks intended for the under-threes. They are, however, present in many drinks that older children and adults enjoy, such as fruit concentrates. These should not be given to a baby.

Baby fruit juices should contain only fruit sugars (which are present in regular fruit juice), although you could get the same result for less cost by diluting "adult" fruit juices or your own freshly pressed, squeezed or juiced (see pp. 42–43).

Spring water

Some bottled waters (described as natural spring waters) contain higher concentrations of mineral salts than young babies can deal with. In particular, high levels of nitrates, sulfates, and fluoride should be avoided. Check the label for details of the water's chemical composition. Many manufacturers provide extra information over the phone if you need it. Babies should not be given sparkling or carbonated water.

SO_4	Sulfate
NO_3	Nitrate
Fl	Fluorine
Mg	Magnesium
Na	Sodium
K	Potassium
HCO_3	Bicarbonates
Cl	Chloride
Ca	Calcium

SUITABLE CONTAINERS

From the age of around five months, your baby begins to be able to sip rather than suck and can start practicing drinking from a cup.

■ For safety, choose unbreakable plastic rather than paper or thin plastic which crush easily.

■ A cup with a spout is easy to use and helps make the transition from sucking to sipping easier.

■ Another alternative is to use a drinking or feeding system. This is a wide-necked bottle with nipple, locking ring, sealing disk, and lid, to which you can attach a handle and soft spout.

GIVING YOUR BABY DRINKS

1 Put a small amount of water in a cup, and sit the baby on your knee or in a baby seat or highchair.

2 Hold the cup to your baby's mouth and tip it slightly so a few drops come out. Take it slowly to give your baby time to swallow.

3 As with first foods, if your baby turns away, pushes the cup away or starts to cry, abandon the attempt and try again another time.

At first most of the liquid will spill out. Some babies are so eager, they make a lunge for the cup – and it's best to let them try. Spills are not important, and this is by far the best way to learn.

COMMERCIAL BABY FOODS

Some parents thoroughly enjoy preparing and cooking food for their baby. Making your own baby food is cheaper than buying commercial foods and has two great advantages: you know exactly what is going into it, and it is family food, although less lumpy, initially at least. But most parents today are also busy people, and turn to the pantry at least some of the time, especially when they are on vacation or traveling. There is a vast selection of cans, jars, and even fresh convenience meals to choose from.

ADVANTAGES OF USING COMMERCIAL BABY FOODS

Commercial baby foods are quick, easy, convenient, and safe. They are hygienically prepared to a guaranteed nutritional standard. Because they can be mixed in small quantities, they are especially useful in the early days of solids when your baby is just having tastes of different foods. They are a convenient option when you and your baby are away from home, and for times when the rest of the family is having something that is not baby-friendly.

DISADVANTAGES OF COMMERCIAL BABY FOODS

Using commercially prepared foods all the time is expensive and does not give your baby the experience of a range of tastes and textures. Because these baby foods are rather mushy in texture, they may discourage a baby from developing the ability to deal with lumps, an essential skill. It is also important for babies and young children to appreciate the minute variations in taste and texture that characterize home cooking.

WATCH THAT LABEL

In the past many commercial baby foods contained unnecessary additives such as modified starch, sugar, flavorings, and extra nutrients, both to replace nutrients lost during manufacture and to make the foods look and taste more appetizing.

Most baby food manufacturers have taken on board nutritionists' and parents' concerns about the nutritional value of food and the potential dangers of unnecessary additives. Baby foods are free from artificial additives, and most do not contain added salt, sugar, or preservatives. But it is worth reading labels in detail. Ingredients are listed in order of the largest quantity first, so avoid any foods that contain "empty calorie ingredients" like sugar or water first.

DO'S AND DON'TS OF USING COMMERCIAL FOOD

Do:

- Check the ingredients listed on the label.

- Watch out for potential allergy-provoking foods such as egg whites, citrus fruits, and tomatoes in the first year and anything containing gluten (found in wheat, oats, rye, and barley) before six months.

- Follow heating and serving preparations carefully.

- If you think your baby is not going to finish a whole jar or can, put an appropriate amount in a bowl and store the rest in the refrigerator.

Don't:

- Store unused food in cans or jars. Instead, transfer the food you won't use to a covered bowl and store in the refrigerator.

- Keep opened food for longer than 48 hours or as recommended by the manufacturer.

- Feed your baby straight from the can or jar unless he is going to eat the entire contents at one meal: bacteria from his saliva could contaminate the food.

- Restrict the range of foods your baby eats, even if some go down better than others. Babies need to experience a variety of tastes and textures.

MIX AND MATCH

One of the most successful ways to use commercial foods is to combine them with your own homemade food. Some of the most useful purchased foods are those which contain a single ingredient – such as meat or a vegetable – as they can easily be combined with homemade foods.

Baby rice is a convenient first food, and it is also useful once your baby has begun to eat a wider variety of foods (see pp. 28–29). Mix it with fruit and vegetables for added interest; for example, puree a canned apricot and stir it into the rice, mash up a banana, or stir in a little pureed apple or pear. For a nonsweet taste, mix rice with carrot or pea puree or some meat juices.

Fruit puree in cans and jars is another versatile product. Use it mixed into a yogurt. Once your baby is eating a more varied diet, add a little cooked meat, fish, or grated cheese to some reconstituted dried vegetable mix or a jar of vegetable puree.

MIXED DINNERS

"Mixed dinners" (meat or fish, plus potato or rice and a vegetable, for example) from cans and jars often contain less protein, iron, and other nutrients than a home-cooked mixed meal. If you want to combine meat and vegetables, for example, buy them separately and mix them yourself. Fresh convenience meals from the refrigerator cabinet are a recent innovation. These are more similar in taste and texture to "real" foods. Most can be microwaved – take care to stir thoroughly – and many are suitable for home freezing.

BROADENING THE DIET

As your baby becomes more familiar with solids and begins to eat larger quantities of food, start to introduce a wider variety of tastes and textures. Exactly what you offer may depend on the foods that are in season and what you and your family normally eat. If some of the foods you eat are not mentioned in the pages that follow, check with your pediatrician if you have doubts about their suitability. However, try not to restrict your baby's diet solely to the foods that the rest of your family eats. Food tastes are established very early in life. As a parent you have an important role to play in helping your child to enjoy as wide a range of nutritious and healthy foods as possible.

NEW FOODS TO TRY

Besides baby rice, your baby may now like to try cornmeal, tapioca, or millet – but no oats, barley, rye, or wheat until he is six months old. If there is no history of allergy in your family, you can also gradually introduce dairy products in small amounts. Try natural unsweetened yogurt. A little homemade milk-based sauce (use whole milk and cornstarch with a small amount of chopped parsley or mild cheddar cheese) is also worth trying. Serve with mashed or pureed cauliflower or potato.

Don't worry if your baby rejects a new food when you first offer it. Simply try again another day or mix it with a food that you know your baby enjoys.

Allergic reactions

The following may be signs of food or other allergies. If you suspect an allergic reaction, ask to be referred to a dietician specializing in children's nutrition.

■ Runny nose, sneezing, wheezing, watering eyes, persistent cough, recurrent ear infection.

■ Dry, red, scaly rash on the face or in the crease of the neck.

■ Swollen lips, puffy eyelids, or swollen hands and feet.

■ Diarrhea with mucus, constipation, bloating, excessive gas.

■ Excessive spitting up.

■ Poor weight gain.

For more on allergies see pages 96–99.

COMBINATIONS TO TRY

- Parsnip and apple
- Parsnip and pea
- Potato and broccoli
- Potato and apple
- Potato and spinach
- Cauliflower and carrot
- Carrot and potato

- Sweet potato and parsnip
- Sweet potato and apple
- Cauliflower and broccoli
- Zucchini and banana

- Spinach and banana
- Avocado and papaya
- Banana and orange juice
- Apricot and pear
- Melon, steamed and pureed
- Kiwi and banana
- Apple and raspberry
- Mango, mashed or pureed

NEW COMBINATIONS

Once your baby has gotten used to the taste of individual fruits and vegetables, you can start to mix them. Pediatricians once advised parents to introduce one food at a time, leaving several days between new foods. However, unless your baby is at risk of food allergy or has an allergic reaction to a food, there is no reason to do this. In fact, your baby is likely to accept new foods more readily if they are mixed with something familiar. He also needs to experience as wide a variety of different foods as possible. You may even find your baby enjoys combinations of foods that you find rather strange.

CHANGING TEXTURES

You should also gradually start to make foods for your baby thicker in consistency and lumpier in texture. Try mashing cooked vegetables rather than pureeing or straining them. You can always thicken runny purees by adding a little baby rice, cooked potato, sweet potato, or banana.

WEANING PATTERNS

Every baby is an individual. Some take to solids readily; others are more cautious. Some like a variety of foods right away; others prefer baby rice and a couple of fruit purees until they are used to the whole idea of feeding from a spoon. Generally, however, the later you leave the introduction of solids, the faster the transition to them is likely to be. And the more relaxed you are, the smoother weaning will be.

SAMPLE FEEDING PATTERN

This chart shows a typical feeding pattern at four to six months of age. It is intended to offer suggestions as to how weaning may proceed at this age. All babies are different, so be guided by your baby's appetite rather than sticking to rigid rules or taking account of what friends' babies may be doing.

	On waking	Breakfast time	Midmorning
Baby aged four months	breast or bottle feed	breast or bottle feed	breast or bottle feed
Baby aged four and a half months	breast or bottle feed	breast or bottle feed; mashed banana	breast or bottle feed
Baby aged five months	breast or bottle feed	breast or bottle feed; baby rice	breast or bottle feed
Baby aged five and a half months	breast or bottle feed	breast or bottle feed; baby cereal with mixed fruit puree	
Baby aged six months	breast or bottle feed	breast or bottle feed; baby cereal; yogurt	

THE IMPORTANCE OF MILK

Milk remains your baby's major source of nourishment. If you are breast-feeding, let your baby feed for as long as he wants. If you are bottle-feeding part of the time and breast-feeding at others – if you have returned to work, for example – you may be able to keep the early morning and bedtime breast-feeds going. A bottle-fed baby needs about a pint (500 ml) of formula a day.

Lunchtime	Suppertime	Before bed
breast or bottle feed; baby rice cereal	breast or bottle feed	breast or bottle feed
potato puree; drink of cooled boiled water	breast or bottle- feed	breast or bottle feed
carrot and potato puree; drink of cooled boiled water	papaya puree; drink of cooled boiled water	breast or bottle feed
zucchini and carrot puree; drink of cooled boiled water	apple puree with baby rice; drink of cooled boiled water	breast or bottle feed
cauliflower puree with parsley sauce; drink of cooled boiled water	mashed banana; drink of cooled boiled water	breast or bottle feed

PROBLEM SOLVING

Some babies take to solids very quickly. However, others take some time to get accustomed to the change from the breast or bottle to "proper" food. Don't rush – let your baby set the pace of weaning and the introduction and quantity of new foods.

PROBLEMS WITH SOLIDS

Most so-called problems are not problems at all, but a normal part of weaning as your baby gets used to taking food from a spoon. However, reluctance to take solids is sometimes due to a minor illness or to teething. See your doctor if you suspect an illness; try a teething gel on sore gums. Food refusal, spitting food out, vomiting it up, demanding something else, or demanding to be fed more slowly or quickly are all normal. You will find more information on specific food problems in Chapter 6. In the meantime:

■ Have patience and give your baby time and encouragement.

■ If your baby really doesn't seem to take to solids, try leaving them out for a week or so and then try again.

■ Milk still remains a vital part of your baby's diet for the first six to nine months so, as long as breast or bottle feeds continue, you can rest assured that your baby is getting enough nourishment. If you are worried, have a word with your pediatrician.

■ Sometimes a baby wants to go back exclusively to breast milk or formula. This often happens during a minor illness (see pp. 108–109), and normal appetite and interest in solid foods return when the illness is over.

■ If your baby is not ill, continue to offer a variety of foods from a spoon. Never put solids in a bottle. And never force a baby to eat solids or to continue eating after he has lost interest in them.

■ Do not assume that a rejected food is permanently off the menu: babies have short memories and may eat with relish today what they spat out yesterday.

■ Stay relaxed. If waste upsets you, don't spend hours lovingly preparing food. Tension communicates itself, and your baby will pick up on any anxieties you have.

Toward Family Meals

DAILY NEEDS

	Starchy foods	Fruits/vegetables	Proteins
6–9 months	2–3 servings	2 servings	1 serving
9–12 months	3–4 servings	3–4 servings	1–2 servings

Quantities

Your baby will gradually eat larger quantities of food – though in deciding precisely how much, you should be guided by your baby's appetite. Never force extra food on your baby. In addition to the guide to quantities of solid food, your baby should have about 1 pint (500 ml) of breast or formula milk a day.

A serving is a slice of bread, a small bowl of cereal, or a small baked potato; an apple, pear or banana, carrot, or couple of broccoli or cauliflower flowerets; and 1 ounce (25 g) meat or fish or 2 ounces (50 g) lentils.

YOUR BABY'S NUTRITIONAL NEEDS

It is never too early to start planning your baby's diet around sound nutritional principles. Offer your baby as large a variety of foods as she accepts, but remember that a healthy high-fiber low-fat adult diet is unsuitable for a small child's digestive system and energy requirements. Try to make sure your baby has some of the following every day:

■ **Fruits and vegetables:** fruits and vegetables are an important source of vitamins, minerals, trace elements (nutrients that are important but only available in small amounts), and fiber. Important vitamins for babies and young children include vitamin A, found in red, green, and yellow fruits and vegetables, and vitamin C found in most fruits and vegetables but especially in green vegetables and citrus fruits, cantaloupe, and mango.

■ **Starchy foods (carbohydrates):** starchy foods such as bread, potatoes, rice, pasta, and cereals are all important for providing energy, some protein, and fiber, as well as certain vitamins, such as vitamin B.

■ **Protein (meat, fish, eggs, poultry, legumes, nuts, tofu):** protein is vital to help your baby grow. As weaning progresses, you should start to make sure your baby has some protein at two out of three meals. Protein does not have to be meat or fish. Dairy products, beans, and lentils served with cereal give a good supply (see also pp. 38–39).

■ **Fats:** children need proportionately more fat in their diets than adults, so for the first two years of your child's life, serve full-fat milk, cheese, and yogurt.

■ **Fiber:** a child's digestive system cannot cope with vast amounts of fiber and, in fact, fiber-rich foods may fill your child up without giving her the nutrients she needs. Choose whole-wheat breads and cereals, but do not add fiber to your child's food.

MEAT AND FISH

Meat and fish are concentrated sources of protein – needed for the growth and repair of your baby's body – and good sources of other vital nutrients. Red meat and liver are also good sources of iron. White fish is rich in protein, low in fat, and easy to chew and digest, and oily fish is a good source of iron and fat-soluble vitamins such as vitamin D and is also rich in omega-3 fatty acids, important for brain development and a healthy heart and blood vessels.

FISH

You can start to give your baby fish from about six months. Almost all varieties are suitable: white fish such as cod, haddock, or flounder, and oily fish such as tuna, mackerel, or herring. Canned fish is convenient, but choose only those varieties canned in water, rather than oil. Those canned in brine or tomato sauce are too salty and should be avoided until your baby is over a year old. Tuna is a good choice – drain it and then flake into pieces.

Your baby should not have shellfish such as shrimp or crab until she is at least 18 months old. Avoid smoked fish and other processed varieties – they are high in salt and may contain additives – until your baby is a year old, and limit them thereafter.

PREPARING AND COOKING FISH

The best ways to prepare fish for your baby are to steam or poach using a little milk or water (a microwave steamer is a useful piece of equipment). Baking and broiling are also suitable – brush the fish with a little oil. A convenient way to bake fish is to wrap it in foil and cook for about 20 minutes. Frying is unsuitable as the fish will be too greasy.

Take care not to overcook fish or it will be tough and tasteless – it is ready when the flesh flakes with a fork but is still firm. Remove the skin and bones, checking carefully for fine bones, then flake and puree or mince.

ORGANIC MEAT

Meat is especially liable to contamination; in addition, many parents are concerned about the use of antibiotics, hormones, and other substances in rearing livestock. However, meat is rich in protein and iron. If you want to eat meat, organic meat may be an option. To qualify as organic, an animal's mother must have been given organic feed – that is, grown in approved soil without the use of pesticides, chemical fertilizers, and herbicides, and without the use of genetically modified organisms – for the last trimester of pregnancy. The animal itself should have been reared on organic foodstuffs, left free to roam where conditions permit, and given "humane" veterinary treatment.

MEAT

Chicken is a good first meat to introduce to your baby since it has a bland taste, is low in fat, and is easy to prepare and cook. Later, you can widen the range of meats you offer – turkey, beef, lamb, and pork are all generally well accepted. Liver is rich in iron and easy to digest, although some babies dislike its strong taste, so try blander types such as chicken or calves' liver. Be careful not to overcook it, or it will be tough and difficult to chew. Liver may also contain high concentrations of vitamin A, so should not be served more than once a week. Avoid bacon, salami, or other salted or smoked meats in the first year of your baby's life.

Always choose lean cuts of meat and trim off any skin, fat, bones, or gristle. You may prefer to grind your own meat rather than buy ready-ground, so that you can be sure of quality and meat content and vary the texture as your baby's ability to chew improves.

FIRST TASTES OF MEAT

To begin with, mix the meat juices from unsalted stews or casseroles with some mashed potato, carrot, or other vegetable your baby knows and likes. When your baby has gotten used to this taste, try offering some pureed meat. Broil, bake, stew, or poach a small portion, then puree or grind with a small amount of broth or with stewed or pureed vegetable.

Between eight and nine months, start to grind meat more coarsely, and between ten months and a year your baby will be able to cope if you chop soft meat into small pieces.

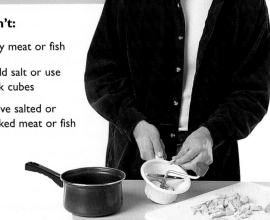

DO'S AND DON'TS

Do:

■ Choose organic or free-range food products where possible

■ Trim fat and skin off

■ Remove all bones and gristle

■ Broil, poach, stew, or bake

■ Mash, grind, or cut into small pieces

Don't:

■ Fry meat or fish

■ Add salt or use stock cubes

■ Give salted or smoked meat or fish

NON-MEAT PROTEIN

In addition to meat and fish there are many other good sources of protein, including dairy products, eggs, legumes (beans, peas, and lentils), tofu (bean curd), and nuts. Small portions of meat, fish, and eggs together with a reasonable amount of milk will supply all the protein your baby needs for growth and repair. However, if your baby is being brought up as a vegetarian or is, for any other reason, on a restricted diet, it is especially important to make sure you are providing a diet that is sufficiently rich in protein.

2

THE IMPORTANCE OF PROTEIN

Protein supplies your baby with amino acids, essential chemicals that are the body's building blocks. Some amino acids are produced by the body, but others have to be obtained from food. Meat, fish, dairy products, including cheese, and soybeans contain all of the essential amino acids in more or less the right proportions. Grains, legumes, nuts, and seeds are lower in protein and contain some, but not all, of the essential amino acids. They need to be combined carefully to make sure your child has enough protein. The best way to do this is to provide your child with a varied diet.

FOOD COMBINATIONS FOR VEGETARIAN BABIES

By combining two sources of vegetable protein together, you can increase the amount of protein available to your baby's body. If you have any doubts that your vegetarian baby may be missing out on some essential nutrients, talk to your pediatrician or a dietician. Vegan babies – who do not eat dairy products – may need vitamin or mineral supplements.

- Baked beans with toast
- Lentils (dhal) with rice
- Hummus with bread
- Cheese sandwich
- Cereal with milk
- Baked potato with cheese and milk
- Felafel (garbanzo-bean patties) and rice
- Mashed kidney beans and pasta
- Lentil soup and bread
- Soybean patties with rice

- Tofu with rice
- Bread and tahini (sesame seed paste)
- Pasta with cheese sauce
- Buckwheat pancakes with yogurt
- Cornbread with cheese

VEGETARIAN ALTERNATIVES

If your baby does not eat meat or fish, try to make sure he has two servings a day from two or three of the following:

■ **Legumes:** Lentils, haricot beans, garbanzo beans, and other legumes are some of the best nonmeat sources of protein, especially when eaten with a cereal or grain such as rice to provide the necessary amino acids. Always follow the cooking instructions carefully. Although legumes are a good source of protein, many nutritionists recommend that they should not be given to babies in the first four to six months. They are also filling and may make a baby feel full before she has taken enough nutrients.

■ **Cheese:** Cheese is an excellent nonmeat source of protein to introduce between six and nine months of age. Soft cheese such as cream cheese, cottage cheese, and cheese spread are easy for your baby to eat in the first stages of weaning and take no preparation. Serve with vegetables or fruits for added nutritional value. Hard cheeses are usually popular with babies, too. Cut into thin slices or chopped into small cubes, hard cheese is ideal finger food. Grated cheese can be given alone or mixed into sauces, pasta, potatoes, vegetables, meat, and fish, or used in sandwiches. Avoid blue cheeses and soft, unpasteurized mold-ripened cheeses such as brie and camembert. Vegan babies should be given soybean "dairy" products fortified with calcium and other vitamins and minerals.

■ **Eggs:** You can start offering your baby eggs after six months. Make sure they are well-cooked and that both the yolks and the whites are solid. Hard-boiled eggs, scrambled eggs, and omelets are all popular with babies. Alternatively, they can be mixed into egg custard and other cooked dishes.

■ **Food from grains:** Rice, wheat, barley, oats, millet, rye, and buckwheat all provide calories, fiber, calcium, iron, and B vitamins, as well as being good sources of protein.

■ **Nuts and seeds:** Unless your baby is at risk from allergy, nuts and seeds are good sources of protein from about six or seven months old. Grind nuts finely or use smooth nut butters and spreads such as pecan butter, peanut butter, and tahini.

Do not offer whole nuts, grains, or seeds to children under five as there is a risk of choking.

FINGER FOODS

As your baby develops fine finger control (starting at about seven months), finger foods – small morsels of food that be can picked up easily – help to develop the skills of biting, chewing, and self-feeding. Try to include one or two at each meal. Finger foods are also a useful way of keeping your baby occupied while you prepare the rest of the meal (or while you wait for the food if you are eating out), and even babies who dislike lumpy foods usually take to them. They also give your baby an element of choice over what she eats and, if you choose them carefully, can be far less messy than mashed and pureed food from a bowl. You can make up a meal of finger foods if you like, but remember that your baby also needs practice with a spoon.

2

PREPARING FINGER FOODS

- Finger foods should be big enough for your baby to pick up easily and free of peel, seeds, stones, pith, strings, bones, and tough membranes.

- Cook vegetables lightly to make them easier to eat by boiling, steaming, or blanching small pieces in boiling water for three minutes or so. Make sure they retain some "crunch."

- The best meats to offer as finger foods are soft ones such as chicken, turkey, and other white meats. Chunks of red meat are usually too tough for your baby.

- Avoid hard foods that may cause your baby to choke (see p. 47).

- Fish should be lightly poached or steamed so it retains its shape when cubed.

- Strips of toast or breadsticks tend to be less messy than bread and butter.

FINGER FOOD CHOICES

Protein foods

■ Slices or chunks of cooked chicken or turkey

■ Tiny meatballs made of ground chicken, turkey, or lamb

■ Strips of sauteed liver

■ Cubes of firm, cooked fish

■ Chunks of tuna

■ Fish sticks

■ Fish balls made with ground fish

■ Cubes or strips of hard cheese

■ Cubes of tofu

■ Slices or quarters of hard-boiled egg or strips of well-cooked omelet

■ Broiled low-fat sausages, patted free of fat (do not introduce until nine months)

Fruits and vegetables

■ Cubes, pieces, or slices of different fruits. Try ripe peeled pears, bananas, melon, apricot, avocado, halved grapes, mango,

papaya, peach, kiwi fruit

■ Dried fruits such as apricots, prunes, apple rings, banana chips, raisins (softened if necessary by soaking in boiling water)

■ Small cubes or sticks of cooked vegetables such as

carrots, potato, or parsnip

■

Small flowerets of cauliflower or broccoli

■ Baby corn on the cob

Starchy foods

■ Cooked pasta shells or shapes

■ Balls made of cooked rice

■ Small slices of firm bread: pita, ciabatta, light rye breads, fruit breads

■ Breadsticks

■ Zwieback or toast strips

■ Dry breakfast cereals such as rice crispies, cornflakes, miniature shredded wheat

■ Rice cakes

■ Miniature sandwiches cut into triangles, sticks, or squares. Suitable fillings include mashed banana, hummus, grated cheese, cream cheese, mashed hard-boiled egg, smooth nut butters, chopped chicken, flaked tuna, mashed avocado

2

MILK AND OTHER DRINKS

As your baby eats increasing amounts of solid foods, you may want to provide new drinks to go with them, although there is no need to offer anything other than water for the whole of the first year. Pure, unsweetened fruit and vegetable juices well diluted are suitable for babies. Avoid concentrated fruit juices and any baby herbal or fruit drinks that contain added sugar.

2

THE ROLE OF MILK

Milk from the breast or bottle continues to provide your baby with essential nutrients for the whole of the first year of life. As the amounts of solids increase, milk gradually becomes less important; but even at the age of one year, your child should still be getting at least half of the calories she needs from milk. Give your baby 1 pint (500 ml) of breast or formula milk a day.

Ordinary cow's milk should not be given as a main drink until your baby is over a year because it does not contain enough iron or vitamin D. You can, however, use pasteurized cow's milk in sauces and milk puddings or for pouring over breakfast cereals. Choose full-fat milk for your baby even if the rest of the family does not use it. Skim and low-fat milk is too low in calories and do not contain enough vitamin A or D for babies and children under the age of two.

Goat's and sheep's milk should not be given to babies under a year since they are poor sources of necessary nutrients. Unmodified soybean milk and unmodified nut milk are not suitable for babies either, as they do not provide enough calcium or protein. They are also lower in certain vitamins and minerals than other milks. If your baby is lactose intolerant (unable to digest milk sugar, or lactose), a soybean formula may be suggested. These are fortified with the vitamins and minerals your baby needs.

You should continue to sterilize bottles and cups used for milk throughout your baby's first year. Warm milk is an ideal breeding ground for potentially harmful microorganisms.

FOLLOW-ON MILK

Follow-on formula milks can provide a nutritious drink once your baby is over six months old. These contain higher levels of vitamin D and iron than human or cow's milk. They are usually based on casein, a type of protein found in milk. It is thought that babies digest casein relatively slowly, and so they are less hungry. However, follow-on milks are not necessary – breast milk or regular formula will supply all the nutrients your baby needs.

FRUIT AND VEGETABLE JUICES

Unsweetened natural fruit juice is a good source of vitamin C. Use freshly pressed or squeezed juices (bought or homemade). If you press your own, you can make some interesting combinations. Natural juices do contain fruit sugars, so dilute with water (1 part juice to 8 or 10 of water) and offer with meals rather than as a between-meal drink.

Your baby may also like vegetable juices. These are available from the refrigerated section in some supermarkets, or you could press your own. Tomato and carrot are good flavors to try initially.

SOME ADVICE ON DRINKS

Do:

■ Offer drinks at meal times or to quench your baby's thirst in hot weather. Avoid giving anything other than water between meals as drinks may blunt the appetite for food.

■ Avoid giving sweetened drinks or adding sugar or honey to drinks. Baby drinks may contain fructose or other natural sugars. Check the label carefully before you buy. If you do offer them, make sure they are well diluted, and not given in a bottle or offered between meals.

■ Press or squeeze your own juices.

Don't:

■ Give your baby carbonated drinks, diet drinks, or sugarfree adult drinks. Not only do they fill your baby up and blunt her appetite, but many contain artificial sweeteners that are not recommended for babies.

■ Offer carbonated spring water as it may not meet the safety standards set for tap water; some contain undesirably high levels of sodium and other minerals (see p. 24).

■ Give your baby tea, coffee, or drinking chocolate. All contain caffeine which should not be given to babies and children; tea also contains tannin which blocks iron absorption.

■ Allow your child milk or juice at bedtime or during the night, or let her go to sleep sucking a bottle. This can cause tooth decay (see p. 48).

SHOPPING FOR FOOD

Buying food for your baby is no different from choosing food for the rest of your family; you should always opt for food that looks, feels, and smells fresh. Fresh food not only contains more nutrients, but is less likely to harbor organisms that cause food poisoning. Choose organically grown fruits and vegetables where possible since they have been produced without using chemicals or pesticides and are unwaxed.

Check the use-by dates of all foods and use by the recommended dates. Fruits and vegetables should be shiny and firm, not bruised, withered, or wilted. Meat should be lean and have a good color; fish should look moist rather than dull and dry. Always buy fresh fish on the day you intend to eat it and eat within 12 hours. Put frozen fish straight in the freezer when you get home. If you buy fish that has been frozen, do not refreeze it. Fresh meat and poultry will keep for three days in the refrigerator.

BATCH PREPARATION

You may find it easier to serve your baby homemade food if you make a batch in advance and freeze it. This means you have always got something for your baby regardless of what the family is eating. Ice cube trays are ideal in the early stages of weaning; as your baby's appetite increases, use small plastic freezer-proof jars.

Cool food quickly, then puree or chop finely and put in containers. Label and date all foods. Fruits and vegetables keep in the freezer for six months; meat and fish for three months; and any dish with added dairy products, such as egg custard, for two months.

Take any food you plan to give your baby out of the freezer in the morning and leave it to defrost thoroughly. Heat food in the microwave or warm it in a double boiler. Stir well to make sure the heat is even throughout (this is particularly important if you heat food in the microwave). Serve food at slightly higher than room temperature: hot food may burn the tongue.

Food poisoning

Never leave warm food standing at room temperature. This provides an ideal breeding ground for the bacteria that can cause food poisoning.

SHOPPING WITH YOUR BABY

It is often easier to shop – particularly if you are doing a big shop – at a time when your baby is likely to be asleep. A drive at an appropriate time may be all that is needed to send your baby to sleep; carry her indoors in the car seat. If your baby is awake, it may be easier to push her to local stores where there is likely to be more going on around her to keep her interested. It is unreasonable to expect a baby or toddler to sit in a shopping cart while you do a weekly shop. Always use safety straps and harnesses provided on carts and follow the store's advice on which are suitable for your baby's age.

Take a bottle of milk or water with you (if you are no longer breastfeeding) and have a snack for the baby (sandwich, yogurt) in your bag just in case you are longer than you plan. It is not a good idea to eat while you walk around a supermarket. A baby or toddler who sees you doing so will want to as well, and you risk laying yourself open to all sorts of battles of will over candy and chips later on.

FOOD SAFETY

- Never give your baby foods past their sell-by date

- Always reheat all foods thoroughly

- Always cover and refrigerate leftovers as soon as they have cooled

- Always store uncooked meat and fish on the coldest shelf of the refrigerator

- Never put cooked meat on the same shelf as uncooked meat in the refrigerator

2

DISCREET BREASTFEEDING

Whether you are shopping or going out for a social occasion and taking the baby with you, feed your baby before you go out. This does not guarantee that she won't want another feed, but she may not. Most supermarkets and department stores now have good parents' rooms; your local mother-and-baby group may be able to give you a list of places with good facilities for breastfeeding mothers.

If you are going out to eat, give a little thought to what you wear. A loose shirt or blouse and/or a scarf or shawl that can be draped will enable you to feed without anyone being any the wiser. Asking for a table at the back, by an inside wall, or alongside a screen may give you more privacy.

SELF-FEEDING

Most babies let parents know when they want to start feeding themselves, either by grabbing the spoon or by ignoring the spoon completely and starting to pick up food (even fairly lumpy foods) with their fingers. This usually happens around the age of eight or nine months when a baby is happy and confident with finger foods. At this point, meals are likely to take longer and become much messier for a while. As a bonus, however, your baby may be willing to sit in her highchair for longer so that she can explore whatever is in her bowl. Encourage self-feeding because it helps your baby to develop important physical and mental skills. It improves hand-eye coordination and increases self-confidence and feelings of competence.

FIRST STEPS IN SELF FEEDING

At first your baby is likely to spill and play with more food than she eats – patting, tasting, squashing food between fingers, turning the bowl upside down, and throwing it on the floor are all to be expected. It helps if you can bear with this inevitably messy – but temporary – stage with patience and good humor. To your baby there is no difference between dropping a bowl of food and waiting for you to pick it up for her, so that she can drop it again, and all the other "dropping" games that are so much a part of this stage of development.

MESSY EATING

Messiness is simply a result of lack of skill and the natural urge to explore the world. Provide your baby with a sturdy bib – the molded plastic kind with a trough for collecting food is best; make sure the highchair is well away from the wall, and protect any carpets or nearby furniture with a plastic tablecloth or sheet. Bowls that stick to the tray by suction are a good idea as they are less easy to pick up and throw on the floor. They also mean that your baby is less likely to push the bowl around the tray in frustration as she tries to get a spoonful of food.

USING A SPOON

Until your baby is proficient with a spoon, it is a good idea to have two spoons and two bowls of food so your baby can play with one while you do the actual feeding with the other. If your baby has trouble taking a spoonful of food, exchange your full spoon for the empty one to give some self-feeding practice. Try not to worry if more food ends up on the floor than inside your baby – it is normal for a baby's growth rate to slow down toward the end of the first year.

Given a free rein, most babies do not usually go hungry, and they eat what they need. If your baby seems frustrated by trying to use a spoon, offer finger foods instead (see pp. 40–41).

Warning

■ Never leave your baby alone during meals. It is easy for babies to choke and, if they do, they need immediate help. Grapes, raw carrots, chunks of meat, and popcorn are all choking hazards.

■ Avoid giving your baby foods that are too hard as they will be difficult to chew.

■ Do not give your baby whole nuts, fruits with stones, whole grapes, ice cubes, or any other foods that might lodge in her throat.

■ Be careful about hygiene. Make sure your baby's spoon and fork are clean; wipe the highchair after each meal; and provide your baby with a clean bib every mealtime.

■ Babies often have a habit of chewing up food and then storing it in their mouths without swallowing. If this happens, coax your baby's mouth open and scoop out the food with your finger.

2

SWEETS AND TREATS

Babies are born with a preference for salty flavors, but this quickly changes to one for sweet tastes – breast milk is very sweet. There are good reasons for avoiding sugar in your baby's first year: those who do not have sugary foods in their first year are less likely to crave them later and delaying the introduction of sweet things also gives your baby the chance to develop a preference for healthier alternatives.

THE PROBLEM WITH SUGAR

The best way to avoid problems is not to offer your baby foods and drinks containing sugar at all during her first year. She won't be any the wiser and not exposing her to sugar is easier than trying to stop her from having it once she has developed a taste for it. There are very good reasons for this avoidance. Sugar of all kinds – and that includes brown sugar, maple syrup, and honey as well as "natural" sugars, such as fruit sugar (fructose), lactose (milk sugar), and glucose – is a source of empty calories that takes away your child's appetite without giving any nutrients. It is also the biggest source of tooth decay. Sugar has been implicated in the indirect development of diabetes as well as hyperactivity.

BABY BOTTLE TOOTH DECAY

Nursing bottle caries, also known as baby bottle tooth decay, occurs when a baby or young child develops tooth decay as a result of being allowed to walk around with a bottle or cup of drink (even formula, but especially sugary drinks) for almost constant drinking. It is made worse by giving a bottle to suck in bed at night when the mouth produces less saliva than usual. The result is sugar clinging to the teeth. Give drinks as part of a meal or snack and not to pacify your baby between times. Never give your baby anything but water in a night bottle or before going to bed, and do not allow your baby's teeth to be exposed to sweet fluids for long periods.

DO'S AND DON'TS WHEN AVOIDING SUGAR

Do:

■ Serve your baby yogurt, cheese, or fruits (raw or stewed, baked or in a compote) instead of a ready-made dessert.

■ Check labels for hidden sugar (some surprising foods may have sugar in them including gravy, fish sticks, and baked beans). Remember that maltose, dextrose, lactose, glucose, and fructose are all forms of sugar.

■ Put a banana in the freezer and let your baby chew on that instead of a chocolate bar (it's good for sore gums caused by teething, too).

■ If you give your baby cereal for breakfast, always opt for the unprocessed, unsweetened variety.

■ Get into the tooth-brushing habit after all meals. Even a small baby can have her teeth cleaned with a little toothpaste on a piece of gauze (see p. 81).

Don't:

■ Add sugar to your baby's food, and stop putting it on your own.

■ Give your baby sweetened juice or drinks (remember to read the labels carefully). Pure, freshly squeezed fruit juices that have been well diluted with water are much better for your baby.

■ Offer your baby carbonated drinks – they can erode tooth enamel and cause tooth decay.

■ Offer candy, cookies, or cake as a reward for good behavior, or offer a sweet dessert as a reward for a clean plate.

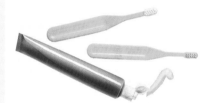

HEALTHY SNACKS

A ban on sugar does not have to mean no treats. Instead of cookies and candy, however, offer your baby healthy, nutritious snacks such as an apple, carrot, or banana. There are also plenty of healthy favorites such as muffins, pancakes, or potato cakes, that you can offer instead of cakes.

Once your child has had her first birthday, it may be harder to avoid sweet things, especially if she has older siblings or doting grandparents who shower her with sweet treats. However, it is still worth keeping sugary foods to a minimum. It helps to cook your own, if you can; that way you can control how much sugar they contain. There many sorts of low-sugar cookies and cakes that use dried fruits such as raisins or apricots to add sweetness. Good varieties to try include carrot cake or apple and raisin muffins.

MENU PLANNING

The menu plans opposite are designed to help you construct healthy, nutritious meals for your baby as she begins to broaden her diet and eat a wider range of foods. The best way to make sure your baby gets all the nutrients she needs is to offer a wide variety of different foods. Babies have very short memory spans, and at six months a baby is unlikely to remember that she did not like a particular food the last time she tasted it. After a space of few days, it is worth reintroducing a food that was rejected: you may find that your baby now eats it with relish.

2

HOW MUCH TO OFFER

Portion size varies enormously, both from baby to baby and day to day. As a general rule, offer small amounts, then give more if your baby cleans her plate. At six to nine months aim to provide your baby with two to three servings a day of starchy, carbohydrate foods (a small baked potato, or 1 oz./ 30 g rice or pasta), two servings a day of fruits and vegetables (a banana, a small apple or pear, a carrot, half a dozen green beans) and one serving a day of meat, fish, or vegetable sources of protein (1 oz./25 g meat, fish, or cheese, 1 egg, 2 oz./50 g lentils or baked beans), as well as 1 pint (500 ml) of breast or bottle milk.

Between nine and 12 months your baby should be having three to four servings a day of starchy foods, three to four of vegetables and fruits, and a minimum of one serving of meat or fish or two servings of vegetable proteins with 1 pint (500–600 ml) breast or baby milk.

MENU PLANS FOR THE FIRST YEAR

Six to nine months

Breakfast

Cereal with milk and fruit

Midmorning

Milk

Lunchtime

Pureed meat, fish, or lentils with vegetables; fruit; water to drink

Midafternoon

Milk

Suppertime

Vegetable dish made with nonmeat protein; fruits; water to drink

Before bed

Milk from bottle or breast

Nine to 12 months

Breakfast

Bread, toast, zwieback or cereal; yogurt and fruit; milk from a cup

Midmorning

Milk from a cup

Lunchtime

Chopped chicken with homemade gravy or garbanzo beans with rice; selection of vegetables cut into strips; banana and homemade custard; water from a cup

Late afternoon

Suppertime

Pasta with cheese; sliced tomato; milk from a cup

Dinner

Miniature sandwiches; fruits; fresh fruit juice

Before bed

Milk from bottle or breast

PROBLEM SOLVING

Most babies adapt readily to the gradual introduction of family foods and the gradual lessening of the nourishment derived from milk. These are the most common problems you may encounter.

LACK OF APPETITE

Your baby's weight gain slows after the age of six months, so it is possible to worry unnecessarily about a lack of appetite. Given a reasonable selection of food, no baby willingly starves. Milk may dent the appetite for food, but don't restrict your baby's milk intake: it is still a major source of nourishment. Make sure you do not offer endless food between meals to make up for what she isn't eating at mealtimes. Don't worry if your baby goes on food kicks, eating only one particular food. Go along with it (but continue to offer other foods), and your baby will eventually start to eat a wider variety.

REFUSING TO EAT LUMPS

Encourage chewing by gradually making the food you offer more lumpy in texture. Most babies prefer brightly colored, interesting-looking food to a mushy mixture with lumps in it – so try to provide separate little piles of cooked vegetables, meat, or cheese rather than a mushy mess. And offer finger foods. Do not get anxious or worried about feeding as your baby may pick up on this. If you provide enough variety, natural curiosity takes care of the rest.

REFUSING TO DRINK FROM A CUP

Most babies still have a strong need to suck, so although it is a good idea to introduce a cup in readiness for weaning from the bottle or breast, don't let it become an issue. If it does, remove the cup for a couple of weeks and then reintroduce it or try a different one. A cup with a spout is useful at mealtimes though some babies dislike them if the liquid flows out too fast – check the holes in the spout and if necessary buy a different sort. Your baby may prefer to drink from a "proper" cup like the rest of the family, so you could take the lid off. As long as your baby's diapers are normally wet, she is getting enough fluid.

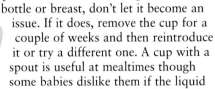

Feeding a Toddler

FEEDING A TODDLER

Between the ages of one and three years, your baby really becomes one of the family. At twelve months a baby is usually still being bottle- or breastfed; by three, this is a thing of the past and the whole family is enjoying the same foods. Use the opportunity to try out different food experiences: chewy, crisp, and soft; high calorie and low calorie; sharp and mild; convenience and home-made foods. Vary ways of cooking, too – boil, steam, broil, stir fry, microwave, or serve raw. In this way food will never be boring for you, your child, or the rest of the family.

3

FROM ONE TO THREE

Babies have an extremely rapid growth rate, but after 12 months you are likely to find that your child's growth and weight gain slow down. Typically, growth eases off at around a year old, at about the time your baby starts to walk and become more active. From two or three years old, weight gain is at a steady, level rate, which continues until your baby becomes a teenager.

Between the ages of one and three, toddlers' physical, intellectual, and social abilities expand by leaps and bounds. They become less dependent and begin to master an increasing number of skills. During this period your child becomes increasingly competent in self-feeding and may develop (and express) definite preferences over food.

AVOIDING FOOD BATTLES

All too often a child's growing independence reveals itself in tantrums over food. This, after all, is an area in which your child can express preferences in a life that is still largely dominated by adult rules. Do not get embroiled in battles over food. Many toddlers seem to lose interest in eating at this age, and this is usually not a cause for concern. Children's appetites fluctuate from day to day, and the sum total of what your child eats over the course of a week is more important than what happens in just one day.

For a toddler, eating is often an unwelcome intrusion into the main business of life, which is playing. And play, after all, is the way in which your child explores the world and develops new skills. If you can make mealtimes an opportunity for play, learning, and socializing, your child is likely to want to sit at the table with you and the rest of the family, enjoy the food he eats there and value this time as much as any other when he has your full attention.

NUTRITIONAL NEEDS

Your child's diet should supply a good balance of all the main nutrients: protein, carbohydrates (starches), fats, and fruit and vegetables to make sure he gets all the vitamins and minerals he needs. Exact amounts needed vary – one child can be a great deal more active than another – but as a rule of thumb, between ages one and three your child's diet should supply around 45–50 calories for every pound (half kilo) of weight. Children need proportionally more protein than adults to cater for growth – around ½ oz of protein a day between the ages of one and three. Around ¼ oz of this total should be high-quality protein of the type obtained from animal and concentrated vegetarian sources. The rest can be from cereal, bread, and less concentrated foods.

PROTEIN IN COMMON FOODS

The following foods all supply around 6 g of protein
I egg
I oz. (25 g) lean meat
I oz. (25 g) hard cheese
4 oz. (100 g) baked beans
4 oz. (100 g) lentils

3

DAILY FOOD NEEDS – ONE TO THREE YEARS OLD

What constitutes a serving?

A serving is a slice of bread, a small bowl of cereal, or a small baked potato; an apple, pear, or banana; a carrot or a couple of broccoli or cauliflower flowerets; and I oz. (25 g) meat or fish or 2 oz. (50 g) lentils or baked beans.

Food type	Daily amount
Carbohydrates (bread, cereals, potatoes, pasta, rice)	Three to four servings
Milk and dairy produce	Two to three servings
Fruit and vegetables	Three to four servings
Protein (meat, fish, and vegetable proteins)	One serving from an animal source or two servings from a vegetable source

CHANGING TASTES

The best way to cater to your child's nutritional needs is to provide a varied diet. Don't be deterred if your child appears to dislike certain foods – simply wait and try offering them again another time. Your child can now eat an ever greater variety of foods, and as long as food is suitably prepared or cut up into manageable chunks, he may manage practically everything the rest of the family eats. This is the ideal time to look carefully at your family's food and eating habits. It is unreasonable to expect an increasingly independent toddler to stick to a healthy eating regime, if you – and his brothers and sisters – do not.

3

Faddish eaters

If your child is an exceptionally faddish eater, you may be worried that he is missing out on some vital nutrients. In this case continue to offer breast or formula milk to your baby to compensate for the nutrients that would normally be supplied as part of a varied diet.

MILK MATTERS

Milk and dairy products continue to be an important source of calcium, needed for healthy bones and teeth as well as protein and fat. Experts recommend that children over a year should have 350 mg of calcium a day.

Your baby can now drink full-fat pasteurized milk and should be having around 4 oz. (350 ml) a day. If your child loses interest in milk, try giving it in a different way – milk shakes using pureed fresh fruit or yogurt, milk products such as yogurt and cheese, or add milk to other foods such as sauces and soup.

FOODS RICH IN CALCIUM

These foods all supply around 350 mg of calcium:
3½ oz. (300 ml) milk
3 oz. (75 g) cheddar or other hard cheese
7 oz. (175 g) yogurt
10 oz. (250 g) bread
2 oz. (50 g) sardines

NEW FOODS TO TRY

Your baby can now cope with a range of foods and is likely to enjoy a varied diet. Introduce new foods one or two at a time so that it is easy to spot the culprit if your child has an allergic reaction. Avoid foods to which there is a family history of intolerance – such as eggs, wheat, or strawberries.

■ Try whole soft fruit such as raspberries, strawberries, loganberries, and other fruit with small seeds.

■ Introduce a variety of breads, provided you do not suspect an intolerance or allergy to wheat. Avoid very coarsely ground whole-wheat loaves since the bran sometimes causes diarrhea and the chemicals in wheat bran also block the absorption of iron from food.

■ Increase the variety of meats and fish your baby eats, although you should still limit your toddler's consumption of smoked or processed meats and fishes such as salami or smoked salmon. Use lean cuts, trim off fat, and do not fry meat.

■ Strong-tasting vegetables such as Brussels sprouts and broccoli may now go down well.

ADULTS AND CHILDREN

Under-fives have different nutritional needs from adults. In particular, they need plenty of iron and protein. Lean red meat is a convenient source, containing more of these nutrients than fish or poultry, which an adult might choose. If you choose not to include red meat in your child's diet, be sure to include plenty of beans, nuts, fortified breads and cereals, and leafy green vegetables, all of which are good sources of these vital nutrients.

3

DIET RULES

Do:

■ Make sure your child gets a good variety of foods to provide for all nutritional needs.

■ Continue to introduce new foods.

■ Try again with foods that your child has previously rejected.

■ Use a judicious mix of fresh and convenience foods, both for variety and to make sure you do not spend hours preparing foods that may be rejected.

Don't:

■ Give your child whole nuts – he can still choke on them. Wait until your child is four or five.

■ Give your baby soft-boiled eggs or egg dishes in which the egg is left uncooked. Raw or lightly cooked eggs can be a source of salmonella food poisoning.

■ Add salt and sugar to your baby's food.

■ Give your baby strongly spiced food or hot foods such as chili.

FAMILY MEALS

Your baby may already be sitting at the table with the rest of the family at some mealtimes, but if not, now is the time for everyone to get used to eating together. You can start the process simply by pulling the highchair up to the table so your child can see what is going on. Protect clothing with a strong plastic bib and put a clean towel or plastic sheet under the chair to protect the floor. Later on, your toddler can sit on a chair at the table with a booster seat or cushion, if necessary.

BREAKFAST

The first meal of the day is an important one, especially as your child becomes increasingly active. Exactly what you serve depends on what the rest of the family has for breakfast. Suitable choices that are easy for toddlers to manage include yogurt, mixed with fruit or cereal for extra nutritional value; fruit such as peeled sliced apple, pear, or peach; dried fruit salad, soaked overnight and with any stones removed; cubes of cheese, scrambled egg, or other protein with small slices of toast or bread; and breakfast cereal with milk. If your family has cereal for breakfast, try giving your baby an individual pack from which to pick cereal – the box is fun to play with afterward, too. Always opt for unsweetened, unprocessed cereal, which is better nutritionally and does not cause tooth decay.

LUNCH

With family members out at work or school, many families do not eat together at lunchtime. It is worth, however, aiming for one day – perhaps at the weekend – when all the family sits down together, if only for a snack. At other times, either keep a small portion of what the grown-ups ate the night before, or go to town on finger foods. Cut bread into small slices or miniature sandwiches that are easy for tiny fingers to pick up.

SUPPER

If this meal tends to be rather late, as it is in many households, your baby or toddler is unlikely to be able to eat it with you. Eating immediately before bed does not usually ensure a good night's sleep, and nobody likes to get home from work and rush through a meal. In many families, young children enjoy a relaxing bath and bedtime story, after which the adults eat. If you have other children, an early supper for them may be the answer. If this is difficult, try to make sure your baby has some of your attention at his suppertime, perhaps sit with him as he eats, "chat" about your respective days, and maybe share the fruit or yogurt he is having for dessert.

TODDLER'S FOOD

Your toddler can now have more or less the same food that you are eating, cut into manageable pieces. Once he has teeth, don't worry too much about lumps, as your child needs chewing practice. Your child may not like his food as hot as the rest of the family, so let his cool; if you serve everybody else's on a hot plate, putting your child's on a cold one may help. Alternatively place it by an open window for a minute or two. Take care to stir food heated in a microwave thoroughly.

Try to make sure every meal has at least one food that your baby likes and always serve small portions, which is less daunting than a big plate piled up with food. You can always offer second helpings. Keep food simple and attractive to look at with separate portions of, say, carrots, peas, meat, or nonmeat protein. Many children dislike messy, mixed-up dishes as they like to see what they are eating. If you have time, your baby is likely to love it if you make miniature versions of what the adults are eating: perhaps miniature meatballs or hamburgers rather than adult-sized ones cut up.

MEAT

Meat is usually more manageable if it is either ground or cut up into small bite-sized finger food – try slices or chunks of soft meat such as chicken, turkey, or liver. Your baby may also enjoy chewing on a chicken drumstick. Remove the skin and check for any loose pieces of bone. Chunks of red meat are more fibrous and may be more difficult to chew. It can help to tenderize the meat by adding gravy (without added salt) or a sauce, or to cook it slowly over low heat.

3

PORTION SIZES

Your child is likely to begin to eat increasingly large amounts of food at some meals and on some days. However, toddlers' appetites vary tremendously. Some manage around a quarter to a third of an adult portion. Others tuck in quite happily to portions virtually the same size as an adult's. Unless your child is becoming overweight, match portions to your toddler's appetite.

SOCIAL ASPECTS OF FOOD

Meals are not just about getting nourishing food into your child. Mealtimes are also occasions when children learn new skills – and not just the obvious ones of holding a knife and fork. Sitting at the table necessarily introduces the social skills of interacting with other people and speech. The sort of food you eat, how it is prepared, your attitudes to food and mealtimes, and the part food plays in your life and your culture are all social lessons, too.

Your child learns rules of behavior that are acceptable in your family and culture through the experiences of eating at home, in the homes of friends and family, and perhaps occasionally in cafes and restaurants. The best way to make sure your toddler learns to behave well is to provide as many of these shared eating experiences as possible.

SETTING THE SCENE

Sometimes eating together is simply not possible (see pp. 58–59), but often a little juggling of schedules means that this can be achieved. It really does not matter if one child is still in sports gear after practice, or a couple of business calls remain unanswered until morning.

When you do manage to eat as a family, it's worth making the occasion as enjoyable as possible. While it is foolish to use a beautifully starched tablecloth if small children are eating, make it a point to set the table (children often enjoy doing this, and few find it a chore if it is presented as "helping mom or dad"). Keep a set of flatware personal to each child in an appropriate size for their small hands, and make sure best-loved drink containers are on the table.

3

LESSONS FOR LIFE

Children allowed from an early age to sit around the table with the rest of the family quickly learn the rules of sociable eating without having to be taught. They discover that it is not polite to grab food from other people's plates, as well as how to handle a knife and fork properly. Similarly, children who learn early that meals are sociable occasions in which members of the family exchange news and views also instinctively learn the social skills of taking turns.

If you do not have a suitable chair for your toddler, you can always raise the height of a dining chair by adding cushions or towels. Cover these with a dishtowel that can easily be laundered.

WHAT YOU CAN EXPECT

It is reasonable to ask that children wait until everyone is served before they start their meal, as long as serving is not too protracted: carving meat or portioning a large fish, for example, is probably best done in the kitchen before everyone sits down.

Encourage talk. Tell your children about your day and ask about theirs (even if you have spent the entire day together). If, however, a story is getting rather long-winded, gently remind your child that it is dinner time. Avoid distractions if at all possible. No child can eat and watch TV at the same time; the fast-moving images are always going to win out, regardless of what is on the menu. Everyone has their own guidelines on when children can leave the table. It really does not matter whether you let a child get down between courses or not as long as you are consistent. If the adults are lingering over a meal, it is usually easier to let a child leave the table for a time. But remind him that he should come back when you call.

AFTER A MEAL

The age at which children are a real help in clearing the table varies enormously, but from around the age of two, get your child into the habit of taking his own cup into the kitchen, for example, and perhaps throwing a yogurt container away. Messy plates, sticky spoons, and real glasses are best left for older children.

SNACK ATTACK

"Grazing" (eating snacks rather than full meals) is increasingly common. In many families, members help themselves to a snack, order a delivery, or take a tray to watch in front of the television. Your child will learn to eat how you eat. Discourage older children from dashing to the refrigerator at every opportunity. While it is unreasonable to make a young child who is hungry wait for a long time to eat, an appetite for a meal is important. Family meals also mean that at more formal meals your child knows how to behave.

3

CONVENIENCE FOODS

Convenience foods are ideal for busy parents, allowing you to spend time playing with your baby, rather than spending long hours preparing food in order to provide your child with a varied, healthy diet. If your child is going through a faddish phase, it is far better to turn to the pantry, refrigerator, or freezer at mealtimes and spend time taking your child to the park, looking at a book together, or playing together. Many convenience foods have an undeserved poor reputation: some are excellent.

3

Safety first

■ Take great care when reheating frozen food or food that has been stored in the fridge.

■ Reheat to boiling point and then let it cool to a temperature your baby can eat.

■ Do not keep cooked food for longer than 24 hours in the fridge.

■ Do not reheat food more than once for your child.

■ Never put food cans into the fridge. Decant the contents into a dish or plastic container and cover with a lid.

■ Always follow the instructions when heating ready-made meals.

■ If reheating in a microwave, follow the manufacturer's instructions on stirring and standing times.

THINKING AHEAD

Feeding your child a varied diet is not difficult with a little forethought and forward planning. For instance, if you cook the family's main meal in the evening, freeze a portion for your baby to have at a later date. If it is to be eaten the next day, cool it quickly and keep it covered in the refrigerator until you need it.

CHOOSING CONVENIENCE FOODS

The less processing food has gone through the better. Processing removes important nutrients as well as introducing salt, sugar, and other additives, many of which have no purpose other than to preserve and improve the appearance of food. Certain additives are banned from baby foods, but this does not apply to many convenience foods that children often like, such as fish sticks and burgers, or to adult convenience foods that you may feed your baby.

The best convenience foods to choose are ones that are as close as possible to their natural state, such as frozen fish, meat, and vegetables. Many canned convenience foods have undergone more processing and are less nutritious. Choose fish, vegetables, and fruit canned in spring water or natural juice. Other good convenience choices are the "fresh" varieties to be found in the refrigerator aisle such as vegetable stir-fries, simple rice dishes, and pasta.

MAKING CONVENIENCE FOODS

It is easy to make many of the convenience foods that are so popular with small children yourself. Homemade "fish sticks," for example, are free of colorings and additives. Dip strips of fish in flour, egg, and milk, roll in crushed cornflakes or homemade bread crumbs, and sauté lightly in vegetable oil. Mini-meatballs or hamburgers made with home-ground lean meat or vegetable protein are also good choices. Every once in a while, you could also include oven fries, which are considerably lower in fat than other types and much loved by children.

3

QUICK AND EASY MEALS

For speed and convenience, use foods that are easy to prepare or assemble, such as baked potatoes. You can cook them in advance and reheat in the microwave; or cook in the microwave, then wrap in foil for a few minutes to crisp the skin. Sandwiches make a nutritious – and virtually instant – meal. Suitable fillings include cheese, tuna, smooth nut butters, sliced meat, vegetable spreads, and sliced tomato. For a change, pop a mini-pita or muffin into the toaster, split it and fill. With some fruit and a drink of milk, you have a well-balanced meal.

MIX AND MATCH

It makes sense to serve your baby a mixture of convenience and homemade foods. This is, after all, what the rest of the family is likely to be eating. For instance, breakfast cereal topped with slices of fresh banana; homemade meatballs with frozen peas and carrots; fish sticks with freshly cooked cauliflower and broccoli; pasta, rice, or lentils with homemade tomato sauce.

RAW ENERGY

Until now most of your child's diet has probably been cooked food, but it is a good idea to include raw foods, too. The importance of vitamins, minerals, and trace elements found in fruit and vegetables is being increasingly recognized by doctors and nutritional experts as essential for good health and to protect against infections and diseases. Vitamins C, E, and beta carotene are especially important. Linolenic acid – a type of fatty acid found in leafy vegetables – is also vital. Raw food is particularly high in nutrients because it preserves the vitamins, minerals, and other nutrients that are destroyed by cooking. In addition, raw food is by definition instant, ideal when your child needs a quick snack before rushing off to play again. Try to serve your baby some raw foods every day, but remember that raw food is harder to digest than cooked food, so do not overdo it.

RAW JUICES

Most fruits and vegetables can also be made into nutritious and tasty juice that many babies love. If your baby is going through a phase of low appetite or is ill, juices can be particularly useful. If your child does like juice, you'll save yourself a lot of time and energy if you invest in a juicer. You can add nutritional value to juice by blending fruit or vegetables with milk or yogurt in shakes, with a spoonful of wheatgerm, ground nuts, or seeds.

(Mixed vegetable juices also make excellent, no-salt broth for soups, stews, and gravy.)

VEGETABLES

A whole host of vegetables can be served raw in salads or on their own. Young toddlers tend not to like leaf salads too much (they also tend to get stuck in the throat), but there are plenty of other alternatives. Coleslaw made with grated carrots, cabbage, and apple mixed with mayonnaise and perhaps a few raisins usually goes down well. Sticks of raw vegetables such as carrots, celery, peppers, and cauliflower flowerets with a dip such as hummus or soft cheese mixed with tomato paste are usually popular, too.

FRUIT

Fruit is an extremely good source of vitamin C, beta carotene, and other vital vitamins, minerals, and trace elements that most babies enjoy. As well as apples, pears, and bananas, encourage your baby to try some of the more exotic fruits that are now available in the supermarket such as kiwi fruit, litchis (stoned), mango, papaya, sharon fruit, physalis, and star fruit. Easy-to-peel oranges, such as mandarins, satsumas, and tangerines, are also usually popular, but check for seeds.

Fruit offers endless possibilities for attractive presentation – helpful if you have a faddish eater on your hands. Make a fruit plate of contrasting colors, cut into shapes and arranged in patterns. You can also puree or grate fruit and mix it with soft cheese, cottage cheese or yogurt for extra nutritional value. Peel and chop fruit and top it with yogurt, cream cheese, or homemade custard.

SAFETY FIRST

- Store fruit and vegetables in a cool place or the fridge.

- Apples, soft fruits, Brussels sprouts, broccoli, cabbage, lettuce, peas, and watercress all keep best stored in plastic bags.

- Eggplant, zucchini, citrus fruits, peppers, and tomatoes can be stored unwrapped.

- Let fruit such as bananas or pears ripen at room temperature.

- Scrub and peel all root vegetables to make sure they are free from dirt.

- Nonorganic carrots and apples should always be peeled because of the danger of pesticide residues on the skin.

- Always wash salad leaves – even prepacked ones – carefully under running water.

- Keep kitchen work surfaces clean.

- Don't let pets walk on the table or work surfaces.

- Teach your child to wash his hands before touching food and after using the potty. Make sure you do the same.

3

PARTY FOODS

Toddlers' parties, though loud and chaotic, are usually great fun both for children and their parents. If you are hosting the party, it is important to keep a sense of perspective about party food: the odd few empty calories and sweet treats are not the end of the world for your child nutritionally. By the same token, unless your child has any specific medical problems such as allergies, diabetes, or celiac disease that make it important that he does not eat certain foods or drinks, it is not worth making a great fuss about what he should and should not eat if he is invited to a party.

SWEET TREATS

A party may be the time to relax your guidelines on sweets. However, that does not mean that you have to shower your child and his guests with endless cookies and candy. Fruit dipped in chocolate is fun and nutritious and not too high in empty calories or sugar. For a healthy cake you could serve a carrot cake with a cream-cheese and fruit purée "icing" decorated with slices of strawberry, kiwi fruit, or tangerine slices. If you want to serve a more traditional cake, try a plain layer cake with low-sugar jelly and covered in melted chocolate.

CHOCOLATE FRUIT

Melt some chocolate in a double boiler. Cut fruit into chunks, spear it on the end of a toothpick, and dip into the chocolate. Put in the refrigerator to cool, and the chocolate will harden to a delicious, crackly crust. Remove the toothpicks before serving. Try strawberries, peeled grapes, and slices of apple, pear, or banana.

3

PARTY MEAL PLANNING

Planning a party spread is easy if you follow the same guidelines you would use when planning any other meal. Aim to provide a balanced meal that includes some starchy food (carbohydrates), protein, vegetables, and fruit.

■ Older babies and young toddlers usually enjoy it if you provide a good selection of finger food. Tiny cocktail sausages or slices of low-fat ones, cubes of cheese and pineapple, popcorn (remove unpopped kernels), and sticks of vegetables such as carrots, cauliflower, broccoli, and strips of red, yellow, and green peppers, with dips.

■ Sandwiches are usually well-liked by older toddlers and preschool children. Go to town on presentation for a party. Cut sandwiches into fancy shapes, such as boats, fish, trains, or serve open sandwiches, decorated with a food "face" or other pattern.

■ Pinwheels and checkerboards are another idea. Use thinly sliced bread and flatten it further with a rolling pin to make it easy to roll. Cut off the crusts and spread the bread evenly with butter or margarine. The stickier fillings are most successful: try nut butters, soft cheese, chopped meat, or fish in mayonnaise. Depending on what else you are serving, good-quality chocolate spread is another idea. Roll up the bread like a jelly roll and cut into slices to make "pinwheels."

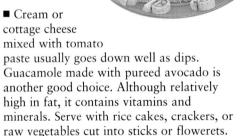

■ Cream or cottage cheese mixed with tomato paste usually goes down well as dips. Guacamole made with pureed avocado is another good choice. Although relatively high in fat, it contains vitamins and minerals. Serve with rice cakes, crackers, or raw vegetables cut into sticks or flowerets.

■ Rice or pasta salads (go for the more elaborate shapes such as bows and shells) with chopped vegetables make good side dishes.

■ Slices of pizza are usually popular. You can make these quickly and easily with ready-to-use bread dough. Spread with tomato paste and add such toppings as tuna, corn, pineapple, and peppers.

■ If you are hosting the party and want to give party bags (which most children now expect), remember that you do not have to fill them with candy if you prefer not to. A small chocolate bar may be acceptable to other parents, but you could use nonfood treats such as barettes, crayons, or small toys.

3

MENU PLANNING

In order to meet your baby's nutritional needs, try to make sure he gets one serving daily of meat or fish or two portions of vegetable protein (nuts, legumes) each day; four portions of bread, cereal, potatoes, or other starchy foods; four servings of fruit and vegetables; and at least 12 ounces (350 ml) milk or two servings of dairy foods such as yogurt or cheese.

SAMPLE MENUS FOR MEAT EATERS

One year old

Breakfast

Cereal (porridge, baby granola, puffed cereal) with milk; slice of toast with margarine or butter and pureed fruit; fruit juice and/or piece of fruit

Midmorning

Cup of milk and toast

Lunch

Pasta with cheese, tomato, and peas; slices of apple or pear with yogurt; water or fruit juice

Supper

Homemade meat or veggie burgers with carrots, spinach, and potato; rice pudding with fruit; water or fruit juice

Bedtime

Cup of milk

Two year old

Breakfast

Boiled egg or sliced cheese with bread and butter or margarine; piece of fruit; cup of milk

Midmorning

Water; piece of fruit

Lunch

Tuna on toast; salad; apricot mousse (pureed apricot stirred into yogurt); water or fruit juice

Supper

Chicken or lentil stew with carrots, cauliflower, and rice

Bedtime

Cup of milk

Three year old

Breakfast

Cereal with milk; bread and spread or nut butter; fruit; milk

Midmorning

Cup of milk; banana

Lunch

Pasta with cheese sauce; steamed vegetables or salad; fruit; fruit juice or water

Supper

Fish bake; steamed zucchini, carrots, corn; pear and yogurt; fruit juice or water

Bedtime

Cup of milk

3

SNACKS

If your toddler has a small appetite – as many do – there is no reason why all his foods should be fitted into mealtimes. There is nothing intrinsically wrong with snacks: the problem is that many snacks are high in refined sugar, salt, and fat. If you offer healthy snacks, however, there is nothing really wrong with snacking, but do not let your child fill up on endless between-meal snacks at the expense of healthy meals.

SAMPLE MENUS FOR VEGETARIANS

One year old

Breakfast

Cereal (porridge, baby granola, puffed cereal) with milk; slice of toast with margarine and pureed fruit; fruit juice and/or piece of fruit

Midmorning

Cup of milk and toast

Lunch

Pasta with cheese, tomato, and peas; slices of apple or pear with yogurt; water or fruit juice

Supper

Homemade lentil bake with leeks, parsnips, and potatoes; rice pudding with fruit; water or fruit juice

Bedtime

Cup of milk

Two year old

Breakfast

Boiled egg or sliced cheese with bread and margarine; piece of fruit; cup of milk

Midmorning

Water; piece of fruit

Lunch

Lentil puree or nut butter on toast; apricot mousse (pureed apricot stirred into yogurt); water or fruit juice

Supper

Felafel (garbanzo-bean patties); steamed zucchini, carrots, corn

Bedtime

Cup of milk

Three year old

Breakfast

Cereal with milk; bread and spread or nut butter; fruit; milk

Midmorning

Cup of milk

Lunch

Baked potato with hummus; steamed vegetables or salad; fruit; fruit juice or water

Supper

Bean casserole with carrots, cauliflower, and rice; banana and yogurt; fruit juice or water

Bedtime

Cup of milk

3

PROBLEM SOLVING

Most of the problems you are likely to encounter at this age such as faddiness over food or demanding particular items to eat are to do with your toddler's growing desire to exert his independence and are not really about food at all. Toddlers also revel in the extra attention that parental worries over what they are eating create. The secret of dealing with toddler food problems is to accept them as a normal part of your child's development and stay calm and patient.

MESSY EATING

It is common for young toddlers to play with their food and to explore it by picking it up with their hands, squishing it through their fingers, or smearing it on their clothes or highchair. Food is no different from any other material to a toddler – it is something to be played with and explored. What is more, although toddlers have better hand-eye coordination and more control over their hands and fingers than they did at young ages, eating is still a fairly sophisticated enterprise. Eating neatly is less important than an enjoyment of food. It is unreasonable to expect a one-year-old to handle utensils with accuracy and neatness. By the age of three your child can usually use a spoon and fork and eat more neatly.

Use a cup with a lid until your child is able to drink efficiently from an ordinary cup (around the age of 20 months). It may help to draw a circle on the highchair tray to show him where his cup should be placed.

Starting to play with food after eating a meal is sometimes a sign that the child is bored with the meal and has had enough to eat. In this case, it is a good idea to let your child get down from his highchair. It does not matter if he wants to return a bit later for something else to eat.

FOOD RITUALS

Toddlers often develop rituals around food, such as refusing to eat a particular food unless it is served in a particular way, always demanding a particular cup for his drink, and so on. The ritual cannot be changed without the toddler throwing a tantrum. Most such rituals are pretty harmless, and unless they interfere with your child's overall intake or are disruptive to others, it is not worth making a big issue out of them (if dicing carrots means they are eaten while slices are left untouched, it is not worth making a fuss). If you do notice a ritual developing that you do not feel able to deal with, try to break it by varying your child's routine before it becomes established. Once a ritual has set in, it may be extremely difficult to break; if you try to, be calm but firm and be prepared for it to take a certain degree of determination and time.

You will find more advice on dealing with other common problems such as food fads in the chapter 4.

Food Behavior

Food Behavior

COMMON PROBLEMS

Problem	Solution
Refusal to eat vegetables	Refusing to eat vegetables, especially green, leafy ones, is very common at this age. Remember no one food is essential, so if your child refuses cabbage, try a different vegetable instead. Alternatively, leave the offending vegetable off the menu for a few weeks then try again. Sometimes preparing vegetables in a different way makes them more palatable. A little pile of crunchy, finely shredded cabbage, mixed with grated carrots and apple and served with a dip is more tempting than soggy greens. Or try ribbon courgettes or baby corn. Make pancakes with vegetables in a savoury sauce, or serve vegetables in cheese sauce with pasta. If your child refuses all vegetables substitute plenty of fruit instead and ask the doctor whether he recommends a vitamin supplement.
Refusal to eat meat	Toddlers often baulk at chewy chunks of red meat and some reject any meat at all. However, you can still provide your child with all the necessary protein from other sources, such as cheese, yoghurt, eggs, pulses and soya products. For extra protein, make pancakes with milk, eggs and a spoonful of wheatgerm. Similarly, you can serve pasta with a cheese sauce or savoury lentils with rice. There is no point trying to force children to eat meat but if they continue to see it served at family mealtimes, the chances are they will try it themselves at some point.
Eating only convenience foods	Some toddlers refuse to eat anything you have lovingly prepared in your own kitchen, preferring the tried and tested – rather bland – taste of convenience foods. The way round it is to combine convenience foods with fresh ones and choose convenience foods with care: low-fat sausages, oven chips, baked beans and canned tuna are all useful ingredients that may tempt a faddy eater.
Not drinking milk	Drinking milk is a convenient way of ensuring your child gets sufficient protein and calcium but it is by no means the only way. Add milk to sauces and foods such as mashed potatoes, pancakes or scrambled eggs. Encourage cereals for breakfast, make milk shakes with good quality ice cream, and try yogurt smoothies.

4

HUNGER STRIKE

The term hunger strike is often used when children go off their food or refuse to eat at mealtimes, although children rarely go on a complete hunger strike unless they are ill. A smaller appetite is often simply a reflection of the fact that a child's weight gain naturally diminishes during the second and third year. It is also a symptom of the fact that an active toddler has more important and interesting things to do: play is the most important activity for a child of this age and anything that interrupts play is unwelcome.

IS YOUR CHILD UNDER-NOURISHED?

Although a varied diet is the best way of ensuring toddlers get all the necessary nutrients, there is no real need to worry even if they seem to be eating the same things every day as long as the food provides a balance of nutrients. If children are growing in height and are within an acceptable weight range for their age, the chances are they are eating what they need. As a safety measure, if you are worried about nutrient levels, ask your doctor or health visitor whether a vitamin supplement is advisable.

KEEPING A FOOD DIARY

If you are really worried that your child is not getting enough to eat a useful way to put the whole thing into perspective is to keep a food diary. Note down everything your child eats and drinks, including milk and snacks, over the course of one or two weeks. You will probably find that your child is eating much more than you first imagined – even if most of what she is eating is between meals. Although constant snacking is not a good idea in the long term, there is no need to worry in the short term, as long as the snacks themselves are nutritious (see pp. 92–93). Keep sugary, salty and fatty snacks to a minimum and provide nutritious finger foods instead.

4

ALL IN THE MIND?

Emotions are closely related to appetite. If your child is anxious – about the prospect of a new baby, for example, or starting playgroup or nursery school – or if there is tension at home this can have a knock-on effect. Children also often pick up on an adult's anxiety about their diet – some refuse to eat deliberately as a way of gaining attention. And it is a fact that food is often an unwelcome intrusion into a child's games.

You are less likely to be upset by your child's refusal to eat if you have not spent hours preparing food. Stick to simple foods, attractively presented and stay calm if they are rejected. Have plenty of nutritious snacks to hand.

Warning

Very occasionally, faddy eating leads to growth and development being affected. If your child is not growing in height, is seriously underweight or losing weight, or has other problems such as listlessness or loss of interest in games or pastimes, seek help from your doctor, who may refer your child to a dietician.

TIPS TO TEMPT A FADDY EATER

- Pay attention to presentation. Make sure your child's place setting looks clean and attractive.

- Use bright place mats, plates and cups and be creative with presentation.

- Keep portion sizes small. For a toddler with a small appetite too much food can be overwhelming.

- Make sure that your child has at least one favourite food at every meal.

- Involve your child in meal preparation, either watching or helping you. Give an element of choice, perhaps by asking her to choose a meal for the whole family to eat.

- Offer new foods without fuss. If your toddler is faddy you may like to disguise new foods with familiar ones – for instance carrots or cheese mashed into potato.

- Avoid giving sweet treats instead of or as a reward for eating something savoury. It may be tempting to let your child eat biscuits rather than nothing at all, but it will not establish a nutritionally sound diet in the long run.

- Choose the right time to eat: try to ensure that your child is not overtired or too hungry.

- Try eating in different settings – a picnic outside, in the Wendy house, a tea party for teddy. The occasional trip to a restaurant or a friend's house is much more fun than sitting at the table at home.

- Remember: childrens' tastes are changeable. If your child doesn't like something, try offering a small portion of it again from time to time.

4

TABLE MANNERS

Since most meals today tend to be casual occasions, less emphasis is laid on formal table manners. However, a toddler who is not told, cannot be expected to know that it is unacceptable to crawl on the table, to take food from other people's plates, to throw her cup or plate to the floor or to smear food on her high chair tray. Toddlers need to be guided gently into more acceptable behavior. If you help your child to behave in a courteous way, not only will mealtimes be more enjoyable within the family but life will also be easier if you take your child to a restaurant or to visit relatives.

INTRODUCING SIMPLE MANNERS

The best way to teach your child table manners is to let her eat with you and the rest of your family and observe how you behave. Try to stay calm and keep instructions to a minimum. Mealtimes should be enjoyable occasions and if you are constantly rebuking your child you will create an atmosphere of tension that can be counterproductive.

TOP TABLE TIPS

■ Try to keep absolute rules few and simple.

■ Be consistent. Don't let your child do one thing one day and then expect her not to do the same thing the next.

■ Set a good example. If you eat with a plate on your lap while watching TV you can't expect your child to sit up straight at the table.

■ If your child appears to be behaving badly, ask yourself, "Does it really matter?" If it doesn't it is not worth making an issue of it.

■ Help your child to recognize that different people and different circumstances require different types of behavior. Offering as many experiences as possible will help your child learn how to behave in different circumstances.

PLEASING OTHERS

Sometimes a type of behavior is only a problem because someone else (such as a grandparent for example) says it is. Consider whether the expected behavior is unrealistic: it is not reasonable to expect a one year old to eat with his mouth closed, nor is it important. Grandparents may have forgotten how a child of this age behaves.

Or thinking may have changed. Many table manners are common sense but some old rules are arbitrary: there is no point in trying to force a child to "clean her plate", or to eat something she dislikes. Encouraging a child to "eat up" by playing games to make him take an extra mouthful can in the short-term lead to food refusal and, long-term, may even lead to eating disorders.

4

WHEN TABLE MANNERS ARE A PROBLEM

Always bear your child's age and stage of development in mind. Banging her spoon on the high chair tray as she waits for dinner is understandable in a one year old but less acceptable in a three year old. As your child gets older adding a simple explanation of why something is undesirable helps her to recognize that rules are there for a reason.

Children's behavior often degenerates if they are tired, hungry or feeling ill. They also may resort to tantrums if they cannot express themselves and feel frustrated. After 18 months, once children are able to talk better, tantrums often diminish. Thinking about why something is a problem and trying to tackle the cause rather than the behavior itself is usually the most successful way to tackle problems of behavior.

CORRECTING BAD BEHAVIOR

If you do feel the need to pick your child up on a point of behavior ensure you explain clearly what you expect her to do. Injunctions such as "Don't be naughty" mean nothing to a toddler – she does not know how to behave which is why she is being "naughty"; similarly, saying "Wait a minute" is difficult for your toddler to grasp as she has no conception of time. Reward always works better than punishment so if your child behaves well praise her. Remember too that actions speak louder than words. If, every time she throws her bowl on the floor you remove it and say that the meal is over, your child will learn that this is not acceptable behavior.

It is important to be realistic and gear table manners to the age and stage of development of your child. One to two year olds are active little individuals with short attention spans so it is unrealistic to expect your child to sit still for long. Usually it makes sense to let her get down from the table once she has finished eating. However there may be occasions when she does have to sit for longer, in a restaurant, for example. Try to provide some distractions such as a picture book or a few toys to make the waiting less tiresome.

4

OVEREATING

Healthy babies who are allowed to eat according to their appetites usually eat exactly what they need and no more. Toddlers sometimes suddenly start to eat more food when they have just been weaned from breast or bottle because they are getting fewer calories from milk. And when they go through a growth spurt, or begin to walk, they usually need more calories for a time. There is a difference between these natural fluctuations in appetite, however, and children who nibble constantly all day. Such children may weigh significantly more than they should according to the average for their age and height and could be developing an overeating problem.

OVEREATING AND OBESITY

Being overweight is caused by taking in more energy in the form of calories from food than is expended in activity. These extra calories are then stored as fat. However, it is not quite as simple as this. All children eat more than they need from time to time, but not all become overweight and fewer still become obese (excessively overweight).

Obesity tends to run in families and if you and your partner are overweight then your child has a higher chance of being obese, too. (The child of one obese parent has a 40% chance of being overweight; that increases to 80% if both parents are overweight.) It is not known whether this is because of an inherited tendency to lay down extra fat cells (which then become filled) or whether it is because families tend to share similar eating habits and attitudes toward being active. If obesity does run in your family, however, you will need to be especially vigilant over what your baby eats.

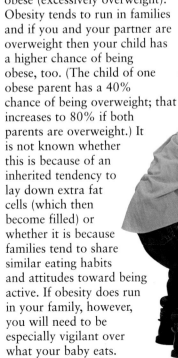

4

TIPS FOR A CHILD WHO OVEREATS

Do:

■ Set a good example by eating healthily. Get poor habits under control now.

■ Offer your child a wide variety of fresh fruit and vegetables at mealtimes.

■ Provide your child with plenty of opportunities to be active. Encourage running around in the garden or the park and arrange trips to toddler gymnastics session or the swimming pool or simply playing with other children. Join in with as many of these as you can.

■ If the measures above don't help, discuss the problem with your doctor and ask to be referred to a dietician who can help you regulate your child's diet. Do not put your child on a diet without taking medical advice.

Don't:

■ Give your child fatty foods such as chips or crisps. Trim the fat from meat.

■ Use cooking methods such as frying and roasting that use a lot of fat.

■ Insist that your child clears her plate.

■ Add extra sugar to drinks and foods.

■ Add fat: use only small amounts of butter or margarine, and try other healthier spreads such as hummus, mashed banana or smooth nut butter.

OVERWEIGHT BABY

A baby who is overweight may crawl, sit and walk later than one who is slimmer because her legs cannot support her body weight. Obesity predisposes to respiratory illnesses. And, although most chubby babies become normal weight children, a few remain obese into adulthood. The best way to prevent your child from becoming overweight is to teach good eating habits right from the start by providing a wide range of different foods. Most children naturally balance what they eat when given a healthy, nutritious diet with sufficient protein, cereals, fruit and vegetables and the minimum of fatty, sugary foods. Overweight children often eat a more restricted diet than those of "normal" weight and dislike fruit and vegetables.

4

OVEREATING PATTERNS

A pattern of overeating may begin in babyhood and persist into toddlerhood. Sometimes, it happens when a baby is started on solids too early, perhaps as a way of trying to combat fretfulness or encourage sleeping through the night. Sometimes it happens when parents get into the habit of using food as a way of comforting or distracting a baby or showing affection. Sometimes a child is offered too much food in an attempt to compensate for an inadequate relationship. Children, on the other hand, may try to please parents by eating up everything that is offered, even if they are not hungry.

WEANING PROBLEMS

The breast or bottle is your baby's sole source of nourishment in the early months but for a healthy child eating a varied diet at the age of 12 months, sucking from the breast or bottle becomes as much a source of comfort as nourishment. Experts today advise continuing breast- or bottle-feeding until your baby is a year old after which the majority of drinks should come from a cup. It is often easier to wean at this point than leaving it until later when your baby has become even more attached to the breast or bottle and has besides developed a strong will. Younger children forget more easily than older ones, too. Whether you are weaning from breast or bottle, you may find it easier if you take things slowly.

STOPPING BREAST-FEEDING

Drop breast feeds one at a time leaving at least a few days between each change. This is easier on your breasts, as well as being less stressful for your baby. Sudden weaning may lead to engorgement and infection of the breasts. Many babies continue having a last comfort breast-feed into the second or even the third year and, provided you are happy with this, there is no reason why you should not continue.

It may help if initially you avoid situations in which your baby expects a breast-feed. If you are used to a mid-morning cuddle and feed on the sofa, for example, try sitting together to look at a book or watch a short video together instead at this time.

CONTINUED BOTTLE-FEEDING

There are sound reasons for discouraging your baby from having bottles after the age of a year. Sucking from a bottle of milk may blunt your baby's appetite for other foods and so prevent establishing a proper balanced diet. Bottle-feeding beyond a year can also interfere with the eruption of teeth and can lead to tooth loss and poor mouth development. Baby bottle tooth decay is a serious problem (see pp. 48–49). Babies who continue with the bottle for longer than a year are also more prone to ear infections.

4

TIPS FOR WEANING

■ It is important that babies do not associate love and caring with the breast or bottle. During weaning make sure you continue to hold your baby close, with lots of cuddles and plenty of attention.

■ Try to persevere calmly if your baby does not seem to want to give up the last feed. It often takes a little while for babies and small children to get used to a change of routine.

■ If your baby really resists giving up completely, continue the breast or bottle for a little while longer but try to restrict the frequency of feeds. Offer drinks from a cup between meals and at meal times and only offer the breast or a bottle at bedtime. Putting only water in the bottle makes it less appealing.

■ Do not allow your baby to walk round with the bottle while playing. Put the bottle away after each feed and do not leave it lying around. Do not allow a breast-fed baby to get into the habit of lifting up your sweater in search of a feed.

DENTAL PROBLEMS

As soon as your baby's first tooth appears, you should start cleaning her gums with a tiny amount of fluoride toothpaste for milk teeth and a piece of gauze. Once she has more teeth buy a baby toothbrush.

Poor teeth-cleaning habits, together with excess sugar, lead to tooth decay. It is not enough to say that milk teeth are not designed to last. At best tooth decay can hurt, at worst your child may have to have some teeth removed. This can lead to problems in the spacing of the second teeth. And, difficult though it may seem to instill good food and teeth care habits in a small child, it is even more difficult to break poor habits when the second teeth come through. As soon as your child is old enough to sit still while someone looks in her mouth, take her to the dentist. In this way she will get used to dental appointments at which all the dentist does is say how well she is looking after her teeth, rather than visits at which treatment is necessary (as it will be sooner or later).

4

PROBLEM SOLVING

All parents want to see their babies thrive and for many this means having a healthy appetite for nutritious foods. But perspective is vital: every child is unique, all like and dislike different things, and most are fickle at least some of the time. Don't allow food to become a problem between you and your child.

1 Don't expect too much. All children go through phases when they don't do something you want them to do. Getting annoyed or upset creates tension and makes it more likely that a problem will persist. If you can accept a bad patch calmly it will pass.

2 Don't compare your child with others of the same age. And try to ignore tales of what you or your partner were like at a certain age.

3 Don't give up too soon. Once you have decided on a course of action give it time to work. Being inconsistent – saying no more bottles one day and giving one the next for a quiet life – is not fair on your child.

4 Don't try to impose changes in eating routine when your child is tired, hungry, overexcited or feeling unhappy about something.

5 Try a change of routine. Children sometimes get into the habit of creating a fuss over food. A change of place such as eating at a friend's house or having a picnic in the garden may distract your child and break the pattern.

6 Never try to force your child to eat a particular food. Never bribe, cajole or use phrases such as "just for daddy" or "just for grandma" to make your child eat food she does not want.

7 If you find yourself getting over-anxious over an eating problem try to keep a sense of perspective. Stand back back and ask yourself how important the problem really is.

8 Don't let mealtimes become a battleground. Do fun things together so that mealtimes are approached in a relaxed frame of mind. If mealtimes become tense, take a couple of days off. Eat out, have picnics, get your partner or a friend to cook, let siblings decide on the menu.

EATING AWAY FROM HOME

Few families eat all their meals at home nowadays. With the fashion for eating out, visits to family and friends who may live some distance away, and the ease of foreign travel, eating away from home is part and parcel of everyday life. For this reason it is a good idea to get your baby accustomed to it from an early age. Eating away from home provides your toddler with many new experiences, giving him the chance to experience novel foods and situations, to practice table manners, to choose from a menu, and to enjoy the social aspects of eating in a situation where his parents can relax, too.

5

ESSENTIAL EQUIPMENT

When you are out and about with your baby, having the right equipment can make life much easier. Many items are now available, some disposable, which, while not strictly essential, can make eating away from home a much more enjoyable and less messy process for you and your baby. If you travel around a lot, it is definitely worth investing in some of them.

FOR BREAST-FEEDING

For a breast-fed baby all you really need are you and your baby. However, it is helpful to take a shawl or a scarf so you can feed discreetly and some bird's-eye squares to mop up drips. You may find some breast pads useful to absorb any leaks (especially in the early weeks). If you plan to leave your baby for more than a few hours, you may need to take a breast pump and bottle, and express some milk to avoid your breasts feeling overfull.

Warning

NEVER carry warm milk or food in a thermos jug as it provides an ideal breeding ground for the bacteria that can cause food poisoning.

TRAVELING WITH BOTTLES

If you are bottle-feeding you can get by with a set of bottles and nipples, an insulated freezer bag or picnic box with ice packs, and a thermos of warm water to warm up the bottles.

A handy item for traveling is a bottle with a click-over protective lid that you flip back to reveal the nipple so your baby can be fed instantly. There are also disposable feeding systems that consist of a container and a roll of disposable bottle bags with a container into which you put a bag of milk This comes with a sterile nipple travel pack – a clear plastic container just big enough to hold a single nipple – which keeps nipples sterile for up to 24 hours.

An insulated bottle carrier is a useful item. These usually have space to pack one or two bottles for milk, juice, or food. Another useful purchase is a bottle and baby food warmer which you plug into a wall outlet. Often these also heat cans and jars of baby food. Many also come with a feeding bowl.

5

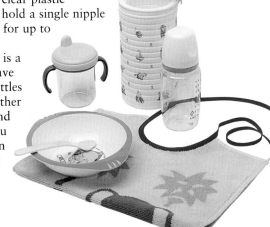

WHEN WEANING

In the early months of weaning, in addition to everything you need for breast- or bottle-feeding, take spoons, bowls, and weaning equipment. A pack of waterproof-backed disposable bibs is a handy item especially once your baby is on solids. They usually come in packs of 20. Look for the sort that has a self-adhesive neck fastening, a tummy tape to secure the bib to your baby's clothing, and a crumb-catcher pocket at the bottom.

You will also need to take a bowl, cup, and any flatware you need to feed your baby. It may be worth investing in a travel set – a plastic case containing two spoons and a fork – to keep your baby's utensils clean and in one place.

Jars of baby food are usually more convenient when you are out and about, but if you want to take a portion of homemade food, put it inside a jar with a lid and pop into an insulated picnic bag or box.

If you are making a long journey by car, it may be worth purchasing a fold-away car tray that fits to the back of the front seat head rest with sections to hold bottles, cartons or cups, and a storage area for tissues.

SITTING COMFORTABLY

Once your baby is on the move, a portable highchair is a useful investment, especially for visiting people who do not have children themselves. There are various types available. The simplest is a fabric chair harness, a kind of sling made of strong material that slips over the back of most chairs and ties behind making it secure for your baby. This is particularly handy if you are traveling on public transportation as it folds up to fit into your handbag or pocket.

There are also various portable highchairs that can be attached to a table edge by means of clamps or plastic grips. Look for one that fits securely to the table and use only on wooden or sturdy metal tables on solid surfaces. Never attach a portable highchair over a tablecloth – it is likely to fall off, taking your child and the tablecloth with it.

Alternatively you can buy seats made of molded plastic that fasten under a chair to raise your toddler up to table height. Take a plastic tablecloth for underneath the chair or table, and you and your baby are all set to go.

When your child is older, a booster seat, which fits securely to a dining chair, is a useful extra.

5

BOTTLES AND BABIES

Make up bottles before you set out. Work out how many hours you are going to be away from home and make up enough bottles plus one extra to cover the time you will be away. Put the bottles in the refrigerator to chill. When you are ready to leave, pack the bottles into an insulated picnic box or bag filled with ice packs or in an insulated bottle carrier. You will also need a thermos filled with boiling water or a bottle warming unit to heat the bottles.

EATING WITH FRIENDS

Your child's view of the world is shaped by the experiences you offer. Eating at the homes of family and friends is not only fun, it provides another opportunity for your child to learn the rules of acceptable eating behavior as well as a chance to experience differences in diet and eating patterns. Such outings can be less stressful than eating in restaurants since the atmosphere may be more relaxed. Knowing what to expect can still pay dividends, however.

VISITING FAMILY AND FRIENDS

Visiting people who have young children themselves is usually straightforward – they make allowances for your child's behavior and are geared up for the inevitable mess that babies and toddlers create at the table. However, if you are visiting grandparents or the homes of people without children or with older children, go prepared with bibs, cups, food preparation equipment, plastic sheeting to protect the floor, and a portable highchair.

DISCUSSING WHAT YOUR CHILD EATS

With a small baby or one who has just started having solids, take your own food supply. However, with older babies and toddlers, calling beforehand to discuss what your child eats may help smooth the way. If it is going to be difficult for friends or relatives to provide for your child – because your child has special dietary needs or because they eat food that is unsuitable for your child – then take your own food. It is worth being very clear with friends and relatives about what is and is not suitable: salted vegetables, for example, or sweet desserts.

GUIDELINES FOR FRIENDS AND FAMILY

It can help to specify guidelines for friends or relatives so they know what treats meet with approval. Suggest:

■ Only one small candy or chocolate bar should be given to your child when they meet. Insist that you will step in if they offer more. Ask for chocolate rather than candy unless your child has shown other signs of allergy: chocolate stays on the teeth for less time than sticky sweets.

■ Encourage relatives and friends to give your child nonfood treats such as a small book, toy, or puzzle.

■ Remind them how much your child likes grapes, for example, or an exotic fruit, a yogurt or an individual box of cereal, or any other healthy snack.

5

A BONE OF CONTENTION

Food and eating can sometimes become a bone of contention between parents and relatives or friends, especially if their ideas and eating patterns are very different from yours. It can be extremely difficult if other people sabotage your attempts to inculcate good dietary habits by showering your child with candy and cookies, promising sweet treats to follow a clean plate, or offering sodas. Grandparents are often particular culprits, equating high-fat, high-sugar foods with the "spoiling" they feel is their prerogative.

How you deal with the matter depends on how often you see the relatives or friends in question, what your relationship with them is, and how much influence they have in practice on your child's everyday diet. If the offending parties live close by, perhaps even in the same house, or see a lot of your child, you may need to take a firm line. You are more likely to meet with a sympathetic ear if you can remain pleasant and explain calmly and clearly what type of diet and eating habits you are trying to encourage in your child. If the culprits are people you see rarely, you may prefer to take the line that the odd cookie is not going to do untold damage.

SPECIAL PLACES, SPECIAL FOODS

Ironically, faddish eaters who turn their noses up at everything you offer often tuck in with great gusto to the same dish when they go to visit Granny or a friend. Try to remain calm about this and not become worried, angry, or guilty. Food served at someone else's house in a different setting is often more interesting than that served at home. Above all, try not to get embroiled in arguments about differences in food and eating habits. Babies and toddlers are very adaptable and quickly learn that the rules of behavior vary from one place and person to another. You may even like to keep a recipe as "something we only have at Granny's."

5

EATING IN RESTAURANTS

Eating out in cafes and restaurants is no longer an occasional treat. For many people, eating outside the home is a regular activity, so it is a good idea to get your baby used to eating in restaurants. The good news is that many public eating places now actively welcome babies and small children and cater to them with special menus, highchairs, baby changing facilities, and play areas.

CHOOSING A RESTAURANT

You will make life easier for all concerned if you choose a restaurant where children are welcome. Save formal establishments with starched tablecloths and waiters in bowties for when your child is older.

■ Fast-food restaurants or ones where the service is brisk are most convenient as babies and small children have little patience with leisurely meals.

■ Call the restaurant beforehand to check whether highchairs are supplied and whether there are other facilities such as a baby changing room or play area. This gives a good idea of the suitability of an establishment.

■ Asking whether some of your child's favorite foods are on the menu will give you the chance to test the sort of reception you are likely to get and how patient the staff may be.

SMALL BABIES

If you do not know the restaurant you will be eating in and are concerned that your baby may not be welcome, phone to check beforehand.

■ Time your visit to fall between feeds when a small baby is likely to doze in a buggy while you dine.

■ Rock your baby to sleep in the buggy before you go in. If your baby is wakeful, take it in turns to pop out between courses.

■ Ask the waiter to heat a bottle for you. See page 45 for advice if you are breast-feeding.

5

CHOOSING FROM THE MENU

Real menu

If you are choosing food from the adult menu, go for simple food that your baby or child has had before and is likely to recognize such as carrots, peas, grilled meat, fresh fruit salad. Avoid fancy dishes with rich sauces, dishes cooked with wine or brandy, rare meat, dishes with uncooked egg, or composite dishes where it is difficult to see individual foods. If your child is more adventurous, you can always give him something to taste off your plate. If you don't see what you want on the menu, ask. Most restaurants have all the basic foodstuffs you need to feed your baby. Ask for small portions – even an adult-sized appetizer portion is daunting for a small child.

Children's menus

Children's menus seem a boon, but many feature an excess of the sweet, fat-laden foods you have been trying to avoid. There's nothing wrong with your child's having these as the occasional treat. However, it is best not to encourage your baby in eating too much fast food. Go for plainer, more nutritious items on the menu such as cheese, hamburger, broiled or baked chicken, fish sticks and vegetables. A baked potato is preferable to fries.

OLDER BABIES AND TODDLERS

Older babies and toddlers are fairly easy to take out with a little forethought and planning. From about the age of six to nine months, babies are lively and curious and avid for new experiences, so a new place with people to see and food to eat is fascinating.

■ Once your baby is taking solids, time your visit to coincide with one of your child's mealtimes so you all get the opportunity of eating together.

■ Waiting for food is frustrating for children of this age since their attention span and patience is short, so take along some snacks and finger food. Also remember to bring a drink in a suitable container.

■ Take a few toys or books for entertainment. Bring them out one at a time so they keep their novelty value.

■ Pick a time when your child is usually good-humored and not grouchy.

■ Give your child lots of opportunity for activity before you go into the restaurant. Although it is unreasonable to expect a toddler to sit for long periods, he cannot run around at will either – a waiter can easily trip over a small child. Check whether there is anywhere you can take your child between courses to let off steam.

■ Go armed with bibs, baby wipes, and changing paraphernalia.

■ Interest your child in the restaurant and talk to him about what is going on.

5

FOREIGN TRAVEL

Children are never too young to travel abroad, and with a little forethought and planning, a foreign vacation can be an enjoyable break for both you and your baby. The chance to taste a new cuisine is one of the great delights of foreign travel. However, most babies and toddlers are fairly conservative about food, so it makes sense to provide a mix of the familiar and unfamiliar.

BEFORE YOU GO

Choose your accommodation carefully. Babies under a year do not like change. Self-catering gives you more freedom to create a home away from home and to cater to your baby's food tastes. However, a hotel can be restful, provided it has facilities for young children. Check the availability of highchairs and facilities such as children's menus and early meals for children.

Time spent finding as much as you can about your destination is time well spent. If you are staying in a hotel, you may not need to take much food or feeding equipment. If you are self-catering, you may need more. If your baby is a faddish eater, the change of environment sometimes helps break a pattern, although it is a good idea to pack some jars of food you know go down well, too.

SICKNESS

There are effective steps you can take to lessen the problem of travel sickness. Don't eat a large meal before you set out, and in particular avoid greasy foods. Encourage your child to focus on a distant point, and make sure he has plenty of fresh air. Frequent sips of water to prevent dehydration may also help. In the future, try an over-the-counter remedy. Don't dwell on travel sickness as you may put the belief into your child's head that he is going to be sick.

5

FOOD SAFETY AND HYGIENE

Children tend to eat less in a hot climate, but your baby or toddler will need to drink much more than usual. Those countries in which fresh fruits and salads, along with broiled meat and fish, dominate the menu are obviously excellent choices for the whole family. Nevertheless it is important to pay attention to safety and hygiene since there is a greater risk of food poisoning in hot climates.

- Always wash and peel any raw fruits and vegetables.

- Meat should be thoroughly cooked.

- Treat milk and milk products, especially ice cream, with particular caution. All milk should be boiled.

- If you eat out in restaurants, check the premises beforehand to make sure they look clean and hygienic.

- Avoid shellfish and spicy foods.

- Avoid street food and snacks.

- Keep formula milk and any opened jars of baby food chilled in an insulated bag.

- Never feed your baby milk that has been allowed to stay warm.

- Do not use opened food or drink once they are no longer cool to the touch.

- Boil all drinking water; if you use bottled spring water, check that it is suitable for a baby (see p. 24).

AIR TRAVEL

Traveling by air is often trouble-free with a little advance planning.

- Pressurized cabins are dehydrating so make sure your baby drinks plenty of water. Offer something to chew on takeoff and landing.

- A breast-fed baby is easy to cater for. If your baby is bottle-fed, pack a bag to take on board with formula (ready-made in disposable bottles is convenient), the bottle-feeding equipment you need, and/or a plastic baby mug, dish, and a selection of plastic spoons for solid food.

- Some airline food is suitable for older babies and toddlers, but it is safer to assume it is not and put in a special order for fruit, cheese, and brown bread or rolls. Alternatively, pack a small supply of easy-to-eat foods such as miniature sandwiches, crackers, fruit, and a bottle of plain water.

- Ask the flight attendant to warm up your baby's food and drink.

- Feed your baby before you have your in-flight meal.

- Don't eat or drink hot food while you are holding your baby on your lap.

- Keep a supply of toys, books, and games to distract your toddler; most dislike being cooped up in a small space with no room to run around.

5

JUNK AND SNACK FOOD

Many toddlers prefer to eat little and often rather than conforming to the adult pattern of three meals a day. This is partly because of their high energy needs and partly because their stomachs do not have the capacity to deal with a lot of food at any one time. What your child eats is more important that when or how often, although it is a good idea to bring your child up to get used to three main meals a day, albeit with snacks in between. If your child eats more snacks than meals, though, you will need to plan them to provide optimum nutrition.

WHAT IS JUNK FOOD?

Food is usually termed junk if it contains few nutrients compared with the number of calories it supplies. Fast foods such as burgers, nuggets, fries, salted snacks, cookies, and sodas all fall into this category. Certainly, children should not be allowed to fill up with food of this type: such foods contribute to obesity and tooth decay, and by denting the appetite for more nutritious food may leave a child deficient in vitamins or minerals.

Most adults eat foods that are not nutritious at least some of the time. It is possible to become obsessive about junk food and so deprive your child of the experiences of his peers. There is also the fact that forbidding something when your child is small may make him relish it even more when he is older.

In moderation, as part of an overall healthy and nutritious diet, there is nothing wrong with the occasional fast food meal or pack of salted snacks. It is only when junk food replaces "real" food that you should be concerned.

CHOOSING SNACKS WISELY

Not all snacks are junk food, nor is all junk food intrinsically bad. There is an increasing number of nutritious snacks on the market. These include unsalted potato chips, which contain some protein and carbohydrate, or dairy ice cream which contains as much calcium as a homemade egg custard. Used judiciously as part of a meal that also contains fresh foods, such foods can contribute to your child's overall nutritional intake. Read labels. The type of snack foods to avoid except on very rare occasions are those that contain an excess of sugar, salt, fat, or other additives. This includes virtually all sodas.

THE PROS AND CONS

By all means ration the amount of junk food your child has. However, if you do choose to ban junk food altogether, be sure that you are doing so for good reasons and not just because you disapprove of them in principle.

Pros

- They are fun.

- They supply your child with calories and some nutrients.

- Children usually enjoy them; this becomes increasingly important when your toddler starts to socialize. These may be the foods he is offered when he visits friends.

- They are usually fast to prepare and sometimes instant.

- They always taste the same: this can be a huge bonus for a child who is conservative about food.

Cons

- They are often high in artificial coloring, flavoring, and other additives and relatively low in vitamins, minerals, and other nutrients.

- They may fill your child up so more nutritious meals are not eaten.

- Too many junk foods may lead to obesity and tooth decay.

- They can encourage an unhealthy taste for sugary, greasy, and salty food.

- They tend to be expensive compared with fresh food.

WHICH FAST FOOD?

If you are choosing junk foods simply because they are quick to prepare or fun to eat, bear in mind that many nutritious foods are also instant or almost instant and may satisfy your child's longing for something filling and "now."

- **Healthy fast foods:** Fruits and vegetables; whole-wheat bread or toast with low-sugar jelly or vegetable extract; baked potato; fish sticks made with uncolored breadcrumbs; canned fish; boiled eggs; whole-grain breakfast cereals; yogurt; homemade popcorn with no added sugar or salt; dried fruit; bagels, crumpets and muffins

- **Moderately healthy fast foods:** Pizza; low-fat sausages; unsalted potato chips; chicken nuggets; oven fries

- **Unhealthy fast foods:** Cookies, candy, toffees, and chocolate; pastries; highly salted snacks (this includes such low-fat options as pretzels); cakes (unless you make them yourself); greasy foods such as french fries; toffee popcorn

5

PROBLEM SOLVING

Traveling with a baby or toddler is enormous fun; seeing the world afresh through your child's eyes is one of the most rewarding parenting experiences. It is, however, always worth being prepared for delays, mishaps, and occasions when nothing seems to go well. These precautions should help you make the most of traveling with your child.

1 Leave yourself plenty of time so you are not in a rush. Everything takes longer than usual with babies and small children, and you are less likely to become fraught if you are not late.

2 Generally, when out and about, try to keep as close to your child's normal schedule as possible. Try to time traveling and mealtimes for a time of day that fits in with your baby's usual routine.

3 Make sure your baby has enough to drink when you are traveling – in hot weather, fluids are more important than food. Take a large container of diluted fruit juice or plain water so your baby can have frequent, small drinks.

4 Provide a few snacks for the journey even if you do not expect it to be a long one – just in case there are any delays.

5 Take any equipment or food with you to make life easier. Useful items include a cool bag, bibs, spoons, plastic plates and bowls, cups, and jars of ready-made baby food. Don't forget any special comfort objects. For eating away from home, there are a number of portable highchairs that screw or grip onto a table, or a fabric traveling seat that slips over a chair back (see p. 85).

6 Take plenty of distractions such as toys, books, and so on for the journey. Keep a few new toys or old toys your baby has not seen for a while and bring them out one at a time.

5

7 If you are traveling abroad, make sure your child has had any immunizations in good time. Pack several sachets of a rehydration mixture – available from pharmacies – in case your baby or toddler gets diarrhea (see pp. 100–101).

When Food Is a Problem

WHEN FOOD IS A PROBLEM

It is terribly worrying when a child develops a problem of any sort with food, especially because food and eating are so tied up with feelings about your competence as a parent. But food can be the source of problems. The incidence of allergies to certain foods has risen dramatically over the past few years. An allergy to food can cause a host of symptoms, ranging from an upset stomach to a perpetually runny nose.

Diet is implicated in some specific medical conditions such as celiac disease, diabetes, and more controversially, hyperactivity. Eating may also become problematic if your child is ill. In all these situations, knowing as much as you can about what has caused the problem and having a practical strategy for dealing with it may help you to stay calm while your child overcomes, or at least learns to live with, a problem.

6

ALLERGIES

O ver the past few years there has been a steep rise in the number of children suffering from allergies, such as asthma, eczema, and hayfever. The relationship between food and allergies and intolerance is both complicated and controversial. Some experts argue that food plays little or no part in allergic illness; others blame food for a wide range of problems. One thing is certain: babies and small children are more at risk of food allergies than adults, especially in the early months when the digestive system is immature.

WHY ARE BABIES AT RISK?

Babies are more vulnerable to potential allergens in the first few months of life because their digestive systems are immature and the gut wall is leaky. This means large protein molecules can pass through into the bloodstream where the immune system identifies them as foreign invaders and triggers an allergic reaction. By the age of six months, although many gaps in the gut wall have sealed, if a sensitivity has already developed, it tends to remain. This is one reason why it is not a good idea to start a baby on solids too early.

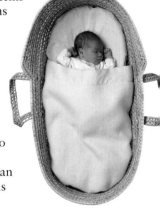

Children with parents or a brother or sister who has asthma, eczema, hayfever, or another allergic reaction are more than twice as likely to develop an allergy themselves (not necessarily the same one as other family members).

IS IT AN ALLERGY?

Allergies can affect virtually every system of the body, and the range of symptoms is wide.

■ When an allergic reaction affects the digestive system, it can cause colic, diarrhea with failure to thrive, vomiting, indigestion, flatulence, constipation, excessive spitting up, poor weight gain, and diaper rash.

■ When it affects the skin, it can cause swelling, rashes and eczema, dark circles under the eyes, puffy eyelids, and swollen lips.

■ In the respiratory system it can cause asthma, glue ear, rhinitis (which causes the symptoms of a perpetual cold), watery eyes, and a persistent cough.

■ In the nervous system it can cause migraines, tiredness, anxiety, and, some experts argue, possible hyperactivity.

6

COMMON ALLERGENS

It can be very hard to determine whether a problem is caused by a specific food because an allergic reaction can occur immediately after eating it or may be delayed for hours or even days. Not all the foods listed are suitable for babies in any case; delaying their introduction may mean your child does not develop a reaction. Common allergens include:

- Cow's milk protein
- Eggs
- Nuts
- Wheat
- Shellfish
- Berries
- Tomatoes
- Chocolate
- Spices

Nut alert

Nuts can provoke a particularly serious allergic reaction called anaphylaxis, which causes swelling of the tissues, leading to breathing problems. If there is a family history of allergy, do not give your baby nuts in any form until she is at least three years old. With no allergy history, you can give your baby nut spreads or butters, and use peanut oil in cooking, but avoid whole nuts, which could choke the under-fives. If your baby suffers an allergic reaction after eating nuts, get immediate medical help.

ALLERGY OR FOOD INTOLERANCE?

The terms allergy and food intolerance are often spoken of as if they were the same thing, but there is a clear distinction between them.

Food allergy

An allergic reaction occurs when the body's immune system reacts to a harmless substance, or allergen, such as food, pollen or house dust mites. The immune system produces antibodies to an allergen as if it were a foreign body. Examples of allergic reactions include asthma, hayfever, eczema, and hives. The first time an allergic substance is encountered, no reaction takes place. However, on subsequent occasions, antibodies are produced which create allergic symptoms. This process is called sensitization.

Food intolerance

Food intolerance is an inability to digest a particular type of food or a sensitivity to it in which the body has a reaction but does not produce antibodies. Examples of food intolerance include lactose intolerance, in which there is an inability to digest lactose, the sugar found in milk, and celiac disease, in which intolerance of gluten, a protein found in cereals, damages the digestive system. Food intolerance is different from, but not necessarily any less serious than, a food allergy.

6

ALLERGY MANAGEMENT

If you have a family history of allergy, your first thought may be to reduce the range of foods your baby has – but this could remove too many vital nutrients from your child's diet. Consult your pediatrician who may refer you to a dietician specializing in childhood nutrition and who can give you advice on all the nutrients your baby needs during weaning.

AVOIDING ALLERGIES

The following measures may help prevent your baby inheriting a family allergy.

■ The danger period for sensitization is the first four to six months, so delay weaning and continue to breast-feed or bottle-feed your baby during this time. Your baby will receive all the nutrients she needs from breast or formula milk until she is six months old.

■ During breast-feeding be careful about eating potentially allergenic foodstuffs yourself to keep your baby from coming into contact with them via your breast milk.

■ Introduce your baby to solid foods one at a time, leaving a few days between the introduction of each new food so you can check for an allergic reaction.

■ If allergies run in your family, monitor closely the introduction of peanut butter and other nut-based foods (see p. 97).

■ In addition to trying to avoid food allergens, you should also reduce your baby's contact with non-food allergens such as cigarette smoke, house-dust, pollen, and pet dander.

Warning

Never put your child on an elimination diet without consulting your doctor first. Although you may think you can identify the problem food, you should never reduce the variety in your child's diet without taking advice.

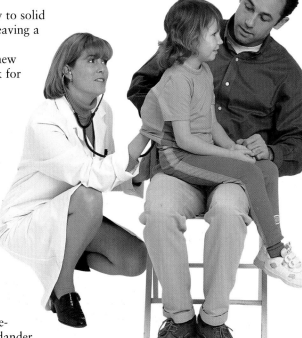

6

SEVERE ALLERGIC REACTIONS

Occasionally children have a rare but very severe, sometimes life-threatening, allergic reaction the first time they encounter a particular food. Red, itchy welts appear all over the body; and the mouth, throat, and tongue swell, causing breathing difficulties. If this happens, seek medical help without delay, and if necessary give emergency first aid. The reaction is thought to be due to a food to which the baby or child became sensitized either in the womb or during breast-feeding. If it does occur, it is important to make sure your baby or child does not have even a hint of the offending food. When the food is reintroduced some years later, it should be done under medical supervision.

A FAMILY PROBLEM?

How you manage your child's allergy depends very much on your personal style. You may decide to take problem foods off the menu altogether, so your child doesn't feel different from other members of the family, or you may prefer to give the allergic child an alternative. Whichever you do, remain flexible and, as soon as your child is old enough to understand, explain why she isn't allowed certain foods. Once she has grasped that a food will make her ill, she is less likely to resent necessary restrictions. Obviously you should always tell party hosts or parents who invite your child into their homes to play about any allergy, well into the school years.

SPECIAL FORMULAS

If your baby is allergic to cow's milk and you are not breast-feeding, you may be advised to use a soybean-based baby formula. Soybean-based milk may also be used for bottle-fed babies who are lactose intolerant. Unfortunately, soybean itself sometimes provokes an allergic reaction. As weaning continues you can give soybean formula as a milk drink from a cup.

■ Nonmilk sugar is included in soybean-based formula, so be especially vigilant about your baby's dental health and stop giving feeds in a bottle after the age of one. You should also avoid giving your baby soybean formula between meals or at bedtime.

■ Ordinary soybean drinks (as opposed to soybean baby milks) should not be given to babies while they are being weaned since they do not contain enough calories, vitamins, and calcium.

■ There are baby milks available that use cow's milk protein that has been specially modified for babies with a tendency to allergy.

■ Goat's and sheep's milk are sometimes thought to be less likely to provoke allergy. However, there is no scientific proof of this. In any case you should not give them to a baby under a year since, like cow's milk, they do not provide enough of certain essential nutrients such as vitamins A, D, folic acid, and iron.

6

DIGESTIVE PROBLEMS

There are a number of common digestive problems, including diarrhea, constipation, nausea, and vomiting, which – though usually shortlived – are often very worrying for a parent. They can be caused by a wide range of factors, including food intolerance or allergy, and, despite their sometimes alarming symptoms, are usually brought under control quite easily.

DIARRHEA

Diarrhea (loose or liquid stools) is relatively common during the toddler years and is usually more of a nuisance than anything else. In babies, diarrhea may be more serious and should be referred to the doctor as the baby can easily become dehydrated. Common causes in toddlers:

■ Colds

■ Antibiotics

■ Food intolerance: if there is no obvious cause such as a cold or antibiotics, think about what your child has been eating over the past few days. If something new has been included, try removing it for a while. If the food caused the problem, the diarrhea should clear up within a few days.

■ Some fruit juices contain a sugar called sorbitol that makes stools runny. Prune juice, apple juice, pear juice, and cherry juice may all be culprits.

■ Sometimes an otherwise healthy toddler experiences repeated episodes of diarrhea in which the stools contain undigested pieces of fruits and vegetables such as peas or carrots. The cause is not known exactly – it is sometimes called toddler's diarrhea or peas and carrots syndrome – but it is surmised that it is difficulty in digesting cellulose, a type of vegetable sugar. No special action is necessary, but consult your pediatrician if it persists or is accompanied by other symptoms.

Warning!

Seek immediate medical attention if a baby under one year:

■ Has diarrhea for longer than 12 hours.

■ Refuses fluids including milk feeds for 4–6 hours.

■ Shows any of the symptoms of dehydration listed in the box on the right.

NAUSEA AND VOMITING

Young babies often spit up milk after feeds, sometimes several times a day. Provided your baby is well and gaining weight steadily, there is not usually any reason to worry. Remember that liquid always looks larger in volume when it is spilled. Spitting up usually diminishes after around six to eight months as your baby starts to eat more solids.

■ In an older baby or toddler, vomiting may be caused by an intestinal infection or by food intolerance. The advice given for avoiding dehydration applies here.

■ In the past a child suffering from infective diarrhea or vomiting was kept off food. This is now thought to be unnecessary: if your baby or child is hungry you can offer plain, bland foods such as baby rice, boiled potato or rice, or clear soup. Do not give milk (except for breast milk or formula).

■ Nausea (feeling sick) may sometimes herald a bout of vomiting, but some small children regularly feel nauseous. Sometimes this may be due to food intolerance. It can also be a sign of anxiety.

CONSTIPATION

Constipation is common in toddlers. It often occurs after an illness, especially an episode of diarrhea. It can also be caused by a diet that contains too many bland, sweet, or greasy foods and not enough fruits, vegetables, or fluids. Rather than resorting to laxatives, the best solution is to increase the amount of roughage your child has by stepping up fruits, vegetables, and wholegrain cereals, and giving more fluids. Fruit juices may also help.

AVOIDING DEHYDRATION

During an episode of diarrhea and/or vomiting, your baby or toddler must get enough fluids to avoid the risk of dehydration. If your child is refusing breast-feeding or is bottle-fed, you should give your baby electrolyte solution, available from the pharmacy in different flavors. The unflavored variety is suitable for babies under a year, but toddlers tend to prefer the flavored version. Contact your pediatrician for advice.

If your baby develops any of the following, which are all signs of dehydration, seek medical help without delay:

■ Sunken eyes or fontanelles (soft spot on the baby's head)

■ Irritability and listlessness

■ Dry mouth, pale dry skin

■ Infrequent urination in which the urine is concentrated

■ Fever

■ Abdominal pains (inconsolable screaming in a young baby may be a sign of this)

6

CELIAC DISEASE

Most babies and toddlers who fail to gain weight properly are not ill, and may simply need a higher protein diet (see pp. 106–107). However, in some instances, failure to thrive is the result of a physical condition, celiac disease, in which a baby or child has an intolerance to a substance found in gluten, a type of protein that occurs naturally in wheat, rye, barley, and oats. Doctors still don't know the exact underlying mechanism that causes celiac disease, although the tendency is inherited, and experts suspect it may be linked to a faulty gene.

RECOGNIZING CELIAC DISEASE

Celiac disease stays silent for as long as your baby is breast- or bottle-fed and is not receiving any gluten. However, if a baby is affected, once you start to introduce a wider variety of solids, sooner or later the disease will make itself known. Symptoms include:

- loss of appetite

- poor growth

- swollen abdomen

- pale, bulky, frothy, foul-smelling stools that are difficult to flush away because they contain a lot of fat

LIVING WITH A CHILD WITH CELIAC DISEASE

If your child has celiac disease, it will probably take you a little while to get accustomed to providing a gluten-free diet.

■ Work closely with a pediatric dietician who will advise you on which foods your child can or cannot have.

■ Be an especially vigilant label-watcher as many manufactured foods – including baby foods – have hidden wheat or other gluten-containing cereals. Ingredients such as flour, cereal binder, wheat starch, rusk, and edible starch should be avoided.

■ Use the wide range of glutenfree foods available.

■ Point out as soon as possible which foods to avoid – but be sensitive. You don't want your child to feel "different."

■ Concentrate on the wide variety of foods your child can have.

■ Make sure your child has a normal childhood – for instance, if your child is invited to a party, you will need to tell the hosts, who will probably welcome a few menu suggestions. Alternatively, your child can take along some gluten-free bread, cookies, and cake to share with the other children.

6

TREATING CELIAC DISEASE

In celiac disease, gluten damages the lining of the bowel with the result that the baby is unable to absorb nutrients from food. The disease is treated by putting the child on a strict, lifelong gluten-free diet, which allows normal absorption to occur and the damage to the bowel to be repaired.

In the past, celiac disease often led babies to develop persistent foul-smelling diarrhea which was difficult to treat. This led to a failure to thrive, affecting the baby's growth and development. However, the number of babies suffering from this problem has dropped dramatically over the past 20 years, while the age at which they develop celiac disease has increased. This is largely a result of mothers following the advice not to give solids too early.

DELAYING THE ONSET OF CELIAC DISEASE

It is recommended that you should not give your baby anything containing wheat, rye, barley, or oats before the age of six months because it has been shown that, in babies with an inherited tendency to celiac disease, eating only gluten-free cereals can prevent the condition from starting early. This delay is valuable because it prevents harmful effects on the baby's growth and development at a critical time.

DIABETES

The news that your child has diabetes may come as a terrible shock. However, diabetes is extremely common in childhood – around one in 500 children is affected – and once you have learned how to manage it there is no reason why your child should not enjoy a normal childhood. Diet and nutrition have an important part to play in keeping a child with diabetes fit and healthy. The good news is that there is no need to give your child special foods. The best diet and meal pattern is the same as that which is healthy and nutritious for any other child.

WHAT CAUSES DIABETES?

Diabetes happens when the body fails to produce enough insulin, a hormone produced by the pancreas that controls levels of the blood sugar glucose. Glucose is needed to provide the whole body's cells with fuel.

TYPES OF DIABETES

There are two types of diabetes. Children most often develop insulin-dependent diabetes, also called Type 1 diabetes, in which most or all of the body's insulin-producing cells have been destroyed. In Type 1 diabetes insulin injections are needed to replace your child's missing insulin. The other type of diabetes, non-insulin-dependent diabetes, or Type 2 diabetes, mostly affects people over 40. It happens when the insulin the body makes is not used properly – a phenomenon known as insulin resistance.

If your child is discovered to have diabetes, she will be referred to a medical team with special expertise. As a parent you have a vital role to play in managing your child's diabetes.

SYMPTOMS OF DIABETES

- Increased urination. Your child may start wetting again at night after becoming dry or start to get up often at night to urinate

- Always asking for drinks. The child is thirsty because of increased urination

- Unexplained weight loss in a child who is eating well and having an adequate food intake

Other symptoms include

- Listlessness and tiredness

- Itching genitals caused by thrush infection as a result of sugar in the urine (especially common in girls)

Seek medical advice without delay if you suspect your child has diabetes.

SNACKS

Children with diabetes also need regular snacks between meals and at bedtime to prevent blood sugar levels from dropping too low. Suitable snacks are the same as for all toddlers and small children – bread or bread products such as muffins, fruit, cereal, and milk.

Managing a younger child with diabetes can be challenging because children's appetites vary so much from meal to meal and from day to day. Encourage your child to eat more regular meals by serving meals and snacks at the time every day. Regular food and eating routines help to establish good eating habits and promote a sense of security in toddlers and small children – whether or not a child has diabetes.

This is not to say that your child has to stick to a set eating regime. With the help of the medical team managing your child's diabetes, you can work out a pattern that suits your particular family's eating habits and preferences.

SWEETS AND TREATS

There is no need for children to miss out on the candy and treats enjoyed by their friends, although like all children they should not have too many sweet and sugary foods. The key is to include sweet foods as part of a healthy, balanced diet. Ordinary candy and chocolates may be given before exercise or after a meal – so long as they are counted in the carbohydrate allowance for a particular meal or snack. The occasional sweet dessert is fine, too. It is not necessary to give your child special diabetic candy, cakes, and chocolate.

FOOD AND DIABETES

In diabetes the aim is to match the insulin the child receives by injection with the food she eats to keep the level of blood glucose as normal as possible. Regular meals containing a balance of fruits, vegetables, cereals, and grains are the key. The doctor in charge of your child's diabetes will probably advise that she eats a certain amount of carbohydrate foods at each meal.

6

UNDERNUTRITION

Some babies do not put on weight as fast as others of the same age. A slim baby who gains weight slowly is not usually a cause for concern, provided she seems happy and is active, alert, and developing normally. However, slow growth and weight gain can occasionally be a sign that a baby or child is failing to thrive due to lack of nutrients. Failure to thrive may also arise as a result of a treatable medical problem such as celiac disease, a heart problem, or nervous system disorder. Feeding a child a diet restricted to too few foods or keeping a baby on breast or bottle milk alone for too long are both causes of failure to thrive. So, too, is deliberately or unintentionally limiting a child's calorie intake with unsuitable "health" foods.

HEALTH FOOD DANGERS

Many of the foods adults consider healthy – such as high-fiber cereals, granola or cereals with added bran, polyunsaturated margarine, low-fat spreads, skim milk, low-fat cakes and snacks – and any foods that are filling but bulky are not recommended for babies and small children. Children should have full-fat milk, yogurt, butter, and cheese until the age of two (unless they are overweight) and should not be given granola and products with extra bran. Once again, if you stick to the rule of giving your child food that is as close to its natural state as possible, you cannot go far wrong.

ENERGY DENSE FOODS

Foods that pack a lot of calories per gram give your child the nourishment she needs without filling her up. Energy-dense foods include:

- avocado
- fish (salmon, tuna)
- tofu
- nut butters
- whole-wheat pasta
- turkey
- eggs
- cheese

WHY BABIES NEED A DIFFERENT DIET FROM ADULTS

Many adults spend years striving to lose weight in the interests of fitness and health and, perhaps above all, improved looks. Babies, however, are generally considered more attractive if they are chubby. This reflects the fact that babies naturally have more fat per pound of body weight than adults. By the time babies reach four months old, they have three times as much body fat in their bodies as when they were born. By six months, fat makes up a quarter of their body weight. Nature has arranged this to provide adequate stores during weaning when eating habits often become erratic and fickle.

From birth until the age of two, a baby is growing and developing both physically and mentally faster than at any other time of her life. In fact, although children's growth rate steadies after the first two years, they continue to need relatively more calories than an adult until they reach their teens. Babies and small children do not have a large stomach capacity, so food must be high in calories but not take up much room.

DAILY RECOMMENDATIONS

	Three year old	Adult woman
	average weight 33 lb. (14.9 kg)	average weight 130 lb. (58.5 kg)
Protein	⅔ oz. (17.3 g)	1½ oz. (45 g)
Fat	⅔ oz. (17.3 g)	2½ oz. (70 g)
Carbohydrate	3½–5½ oz. (100–160 g)	8 oz. (230 g)
Fiber	¼–½ oz. (8–13 g)	½–1 oz. (12–24 g)
Energy	1,370 kcalories	1,940 kcalories
Calcium	350 mg	700 mg
Vitamin C	30 mg	40 mg

6

FEEDING A SICK CHILD

You can expect your baby to catch several minor infections in the first few years of life. Often one of the first clues that a baby or toddler is succumbing to an illness is loss of appetite. In the case of problems such as diarrhea and vomiting, this is actually a positive response as it gives the digestive system a rest. Good nutrition is especially important during an illness to enable your child to fight off infection and aid recovery. In most minor illnesses there is no need to feed your baby a special diet.

SIGNS OF ILLNESS

- Child not responding as usual
- Loss of interest in feeds and food
- Diarrhea
- Vomiting
- Raised temperature
- Crying more than usual
- Coughing, rashes, and other symptoms

FEEDING PATTERNS DURING AN ILLNESS

When children lose their appetite through illness, it is pointless to try to persuade them to eat proper meals. Instead, it is better to tempt them with small, appetizing snacks. Nutritious but easily digestible foods such as steamed chicken, fish, and soup are best, but may not appeal to a sick child. Although junk foods are less nutritious, if they tempt your child, they will provide useful calories, and it is preferable to offer these than to let your child go without food for an extended period.

THE IMPORTANCE OF FLUIDS

It is especially important to make sure a sick child has plenty to drink, especially if there is fever, diarrhea, vomiting, or a respiratory infection.

- Don't expect big drinks to go down if your child is listless. Instead, offer small, frequent sips of clear fluids, such as fruit juice, which provides some calories, as well as water.

- If your child is reluctant to drink, offer fluids in a special mug or through a curly straw – the novelty may make the drink more acceptable.

- This is one occasion when you might offer sodas to an older toddler, if nothing else appeals. Once in a while, the commercial varieties are acceptable – and may be the only thing a sick toddler keeps down.

6

REGRESSION

Babies who have been having most of their food in solid form often revert to the bottle or breast when ill. This is perfectly normal and offers a ready source of nourishment as well as comfort. Unless your doctor advises otherwise, it is perfectly all right for your baby to suck from the breast or bottle.

Similarly, a toddler who has been drinking from a cup or mug may find it easier to drink from a cup with a spout again. Don't worry – once your baby or child is better, she will go back to eating solids and using a cup again.

EASY TO EAT

Soft foods, such as scrambled egg, mashed banana, macaroni, and soup, are all light and easy to digest and slip down easily if a child has a sore throat, swollen glands, or an illness such as mumps.

Fruit is a good choice during an illness as it is easy to digest, contains plenty of water (a way of keeping up your child's fluid intake), and is not too heavy on the stomach, although citrus fruits can be too sharp for a sore throat, so offer them sparingly. Yogurt and other creamy foods are similarly easy to digest and are usually well accepted, although if your child has blocked sinuses, milk aggravates mucus production, so may be best avoided.

GETTING BETTER

Once your child is on the mend, her appetite will gradually return. Don't expect it to be back to normal immediately, though. You may need to tempt a weak appetite with attractive presentation. Even if your child has lost weight during an illness, it is usually regained rapidly once normal eating returns.

6

HYPERACTIVITY

Toddlers love to be on the go, and there can be few parents who at the end of yet another exhausting day haven't wondered whether their child might be hyperactive. However, true hyperactivity is more than just normal boisterousness. A hyperactive child has a specific disorder that affects behavior, learning, and communication. The condition often becomes apparent between the ages of two and five, although there may often have been earlier clues, such as "three-month colic" (crying, screaming and inability to settle in the early months) and sleeping problems. Although the experts do not know what causes hyperactivity, many parents have found that their children's behavior dramatically improves with a change of diet. Boys are more commonly affected than girls.

SIGNS OF HYPERACTIVITY

- Continual crying, screaming, and restlessness

- Sleeplessness (sometimes as little as three or four hours in 24)

- Three-month colic

- Difficulties breast- or bottle-feeding

- Difficult to calm or cuddle (she may reject your attempts to be affectionate)

- Excessive dribbling

- Excessive thirst

- Head banging

WHAT IS HYPERACTIVITY?

Hyperactivity has baffled experts since the 1920s when the term was coined. You may also hear it called "hyperkinetic disorder" or "Attention Deficit Disorder." The three key symptoms are overactivity, a short attention span, and impulsiveness. Unlike a normal boisterous toddler, hyperactive children will display these symptoms to the extent that they severely disrupt their – and your – daily life.

IS FOOD TO BLAME?

The idea that hyperactivity may be linked to what a child eats and drinks has been around for a long time. Children with a tendency to develop allergies such as eczema, asthma, and hayfever are sometimes hyperactive as well. Hyperactive children are often allergic to a range of foods – such as dairy products and sugar. It may be these foods that trigger hyperactive behavior. Evening primrose oil has been used with some success to treat hyperactive children, especially those who are atopic (have a tendency to allergy) generally.

6

PROBLEMS WITH ADDITIVES

An American physician, Benjamin Feingold, suggested that certain chemical additives found in food could be to blame for hyperactivity. In particular, chemicals called salicylates that come from the same family as aspirin, together with colorings derived from coal tar or azo dyes, were thought to be implicated.

Salicylates are found in almonds, tomatoes, apples, and many other fruits including apricots, oranges, and strawberries. Feingold devised a special additive-free diet which he claimed resulted in a dramatic improvement in symptoms, and the diet is recommended by some support groups for hyperactive children. Subsequent studies of the Feingold diet have had mixed results. Some experts think that its success could be due to the extra attention that children receive when put on this diet; others argue that allergy to certain foods is a symptom of hyperactivity rather than a cause.

Many food additives are legally banned from commercial baby foods. However, they are not banned from many of the other convenience foods that children often eat, such as fish sticks and cookies. Additives to watch out for are:

- Stabilizers and thickeners: carrageenan, cellulose, glycerol, guar gum, gum arabis, lecithin, pectins
- Preservatives: benzoic acid, benzoates, nitrites and nitrates, sulfites, BHA, BHT
- Enhancers and improvers: dioctyl sodium-sulfosuccinate, disodium, guanylate, hydrolyzed vegetable protein, monosodium glutamate
  - Colorings: beta carotene, caramel, carrot oil, citrus red #1, dehydrated beets, FD & C colors: blue #1, 2, red #3, 40, yellow #5, 6

CHANGING YOUR CHILD'S DIET

Do not restrict your child's diet without medical advice. If you do decide to try changing what your child eats, contact your doctor or ask to be referred to a pediatric dietician who can make sure that any changes you make are safe. Putting the rest of the family on the diet (which is similar to that recommended for health) will help your child feel less "different."

MEDICAL TREATMENT FOR HYPERACTIVITY

Treatment consists of prescribed drugs designed to improve concentration and curb overactivity and impulsiveness. When combined with behavior therapy to help children change their behavior and develop ways of dealing with it, it is often successful.

6

INDEX

ACKNOWLEDGMENTS

The author and the publishers greatly acknowledge the invaluable contribution made by
Laura Wickenden, who took all the photographs in this book except:

p. 1 Sandra Lousada / Collections; p. 10 The Stock Market; p. 13 Susanne Price / Bubbles;
pp. 17 (bottom), 25 (top), 28 Andrew Sydenham; p. 30 The Stock Market; p. 31 (bottom)
Andrew Sydenham; p. 33 The Stock Market; pp. 34, 42, 43 (bottom), 46, 48, 49 (top), 50,
51, 59, 61, 63 (bottom), 68 Andrew Sydenham; 69 John Barlow; p. 81 Nancy Durrell
McKenna / The Hutchison Library; p. 89 Andrew Sydenham; p. 96 The Stock Market;
p. 97 (bottom) Peter Myers; p. 103 Tony Latham / Tony Stone Images